Dr Kenneth D. Kaunda, President of Zambia, addresses *Letter to My Children* directly to his own family of nine sons and daughters, and dedicates it to a wider circle, the Youth of Zambia, a nation in the creation of which he played so great a part.

Those who have read his earlier book, *A Humanist in Africa*, will be aware of the strength of his personal philosophy. Here again they will find the same warm-hearted serenity of approach, combined with a humanist's understanding of the difficulties of life. The subjects he discusses in this *Letter* include such personal themes as faith and values, self-fulfilment and courage in face of fear, as well as the broader problems of justice and the law, the use and abuse of power, and the long-term goal of a world community.

Kenneth David Kaunda

Letter to my Children

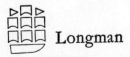 Longman

Longman Group Limited
London

Associated companies, branches and
representatives throughout the world

© Kenneth D. Kaunda 1973

First published in 1973

ISBN 0 582 10127 1 (cased)
ISBN 0 582 10128 X (paper)

Printed in Great Britain
by Ebenezer Baylis and Son Ltd.
The Trinity Press, Worcester, and London

Acknowledgements

My grateful thanks go to those who have helped in
the preparation of this volume – notably,
Mrs Gloria Sleep, my Personal Secretary, and to Mrs
Joan Irwin and Miss Jean Palk who typed successive
drafts.

I also wish to express my gratitude to my long-time
friend and collaborator, the Reverend Dr Colin Morris,
who edited the manuscript. He helped to clarify my
thinking by discussion and amicable argument, and
made a number of suggestions about the arrangement
of material from which the argument of the book
benefited. In the mid-1950s, at the height of our
struggle his part in the struggle for elementary human
rights gained him the name of the 'fighting parson'. I
am glad that he has not stopped fighting, not only for
those who still labour under the jackboots of
imperialists, but also for the rights of man both in the
old as well as the new world. It is both comforting and
reassuring that a man of his stature continues to
struggle for man's rights the world over.

I appreciate the courtesy and patience of Longman
Group Ltd, to whom this book, a sequel to
A Humanist in Africa, was promised long ago. It
is probably unnecessary to state that the delay has been
due to more urgent and pressing matters which have
preoccupied me.

Finally, the inspiration and challenge of my own children and the youth of Zambia is gratefully acknowledged in the Dedication of the book itself.

Kenneth David Kaunda
State House
Lusaka
9 June 1972

*This book is dedicated
to the Youth of Zambia*

K.D.K.

Letter to my Children

How it all began

My dear Children,

Many years will pass before the youngest of you is able to understand what I now write, and no doubt when that time comes you will wonder what made me address you in this formal way. Let's say this letter is a kind of public apology for neglecting you all so badly by putting my political career before my family. There is a Spanish proverb which I have never forgotten. It runs: 'God says, Take what you like. Take it, and pay for it.' Well, that's fair enough. The problem arises when someone else has to pay for our choices. I don't regret exchanging the life of a schoolmaster for that of a politician over twenty years ago, though I have paid the price for that choice in all sorts of ways. What worries me more is that your dear mother and yourselves have also had to pay for that decision of mine to enter public life. Maybe you don't see it that way yet, though you must sometimes wonder why your father is virtually a stranger to you.

Those of you who are older will remember the stirring days of the freedom struggle when I was always on the move, travelling around the country, even popping in and out of gaol while your mother tried to keep a roof over your head and something in your bellies. Now that Zambia is a free nation, things don't seem much better: our family is still in turmoil. I'm no longer on the run, but I am certainly kept on the trot – throughout Zambia and beyond. And when I do get a precious hour or two with you, my mind is on other things, important things certainly – affairs of the State – but it is still time stolen from you.

Of course we are not unique. There are many people who serve the wider community at the expense of that little community – the family – which God has given them to cherish. It is fatally easy to serve mankind in the mass and neglect those people under one's nose. To some onlookers, you appear to be privileged children. And so you are, compared to the millions of refugee children across the world; yes, even children in our own country who have little to eat and nowhere secure to lay their heads at night. But the fancy business of being a President's children is no substitute for a father who is there when you need him – to play with, talk to, or just to love.

When you grow up, you will hear and read a lot about Kaunda; what he did and didn't do; his mistakes and weaknesses – and I hope you will hear a few good things as well. There is almost certain to be a grain of truth in most of what you hear because even lies to be believable must have some basis of fact, however distorted. But I beg you to accept that one mistake I did not make was to forget the sacrifices of my family.

So by way of repayment, I want to open my heart and try to explain what makes me tick – my philosophy, if you like; the things I believe and why I believe them. I won't bore you with the story of my life – anyway, that's a matter of public record. But every man has a secret history which is more than just a recital of events. This is the side of a public figure which the historians cannot investigate – the *inside*. They can examine his papers, read his speeches and record his recollections but they can't climb into his

head or explore his heart. It's just as well. Who wants
to be shown the rust on the inside of the shining
armour of one's heroes? The observer's judgment of a
man is always inconclusive. It is not much use knowing
what someone achieved unless you can measure it
against what he aimed at. Who can share another's
dreams, thrill to his hopes and understand his fears? I
believe that the true measure of a man is not to be
gauged by the state of his bank account, the size of his
popular following or the grandeur of his titles or
degrees. It is a mark on the soul which represents the
point at which he finally harmonized his achievements
with his ambitions, where he settled for what was
possible as against what was desired; not so much a
mark perhaps, as a scar – a scar made by his dreams
coming to earth like falling comets.

Therefore I want to attempt the impossible and use
words to convey the essence of the flame that burns in
my mind and the ideas and convictions which fuel it –
a flame which must die and be buried with me unless I
succeed in passing it on to you.

Faith and values

I write these words in what is forbidden territory to
you, my study at State House – a far cry indeed from
the old mission house at Lubwa where I was born or
the leaky hut in Chilenje from which a handful of
idealistic and untried young men began what seemed
the hopeless task of prising the grip of a great imperial
power off our land. This is indeed a grand setting for
the son of a poor preacher. Around me are symbols of

B

that most desired and yet dangerous of all commodities
– power. And this is as good a point as any from which
to start, with power, for that is what most of my life
has been taken up with; how to get it, how to control
it, how to share it, and most important, how to avoid
being destroyed by it.

The earliest form of power I encountered and which
had a lasting effect upon my life was the power of the
Gospel. All right, I can see you in my mind's eye smil-
ing and muttering 'Here goes the Old Preacher again!'
Well, I'm unrepentant. I know it's fashionable in Africa
these days for quick, clever young people to dismiss
religion as a primitive superstition they put behind
them from the time they first went to the clinic instead
of the witchdoctor for relief from their aches and pains.
Or else they judge Christianity in ideological terms as
an instrument of colonial oppression, fondly imagining
that the Christian God left the country on the same
plane as the Governor following our Independence
celebrations. It saddens me that the clever are often so
foolish. Certainly some religion degenerated into
superstition and, of course, some missionaries allowed
themselves to become agents of colonial oppression.
But a wise man does not cut off his head because he has
the odd sore on his cheek. Leave out the religious
dimension of African tradition, art, custom, language and
law and there is precious little left of our past, and the
bits and pieces which remain form an unpromising
foundation for the future. This *African-ness* about
which so many black people boast and that they
proudly assert to counter the aggressiveness of Western
culture is not just a political force – a drive towards
freedom and racial equality. Nor is it solely a cultural

one, as though one could be reborn into the past by revitalizing tribal dancing and the music of the drums. The *African-ness* which has its roots in the soil of our continent rather than the lecture rooms of Western universities is basically a religious phenomenon; we are who we are because of our attitude to the mysterious depth in life, symbolized by birth and death, harvest and famine, ancestors and the unborn.

The coming of Christianity had a complex effect on this African world view, partly disrupting and partly enlarging it. I don't want to get bogged down in all that business though. It is enough to say that I feel within myself the tension created by the collision of these two world views which I have never completely reconciled. It is a ludicrous and indeed insulting over-simplification to claim, as some missionaries have done, that we non-Western peoples are still deepdown pagan with a top dressing of Christianity. The same could, of course, be said of Jesus who, after all, was a middle-Eastern peasant. The more sensitive theologians are beginning to explore what it means to be Christian in a genuinely African or Asian way. I wish some of our own African clergy showed more interest in this complex problem and put a little less zeal into turning their congregations into black versions of seventeenth-century English Puritans.

However – here endeth a lecture on which I ought never to have embarked. My parents taught me to believe in God, and I have been a man of faith ever since. That is not the same thing as saying I have always been a righteous man. That is for God and my fellow men to judge. But religious faith has played a central role in my life, and even at the price of being considered old-fashioned or naïve I must declare the fact. I believe in a Supreme Being whose love is the great driving force working itself out in those three worlds which interpenetrate each other at any moment of time, the worlds of Nature, History and Eternity. For me, God is more a Presence than a philosophical concept. I am aware, even in solitude, that I am not alone; that my cries for help or comfort or strength are heard. Above all, my belief in God gives me a feeling of unlimited responsibility. What a terrifying thing that is! I am guardian rather than owner of such powers and talents as I possess, answerable for my use or abuse of them to the One who has loaned them to me and will one day require a full reckoning. This sense of responsibility seems to be a great burden but at least it frees me from worrying too much about popularity or fame.

By modern standards, the religion of my parents would seem crude and oversimple. They believed that every last word of the Bible was divinely inspired; that to break any one of the Ten Commandments must consign the transgressor after death to a real Hell unless he were saved by the blood of Jesus. And they lived expecting the return in glory of Jesus and his angels to begin the Judgment. There was nothing sophisticated about their faith, but it was real and strong and wholesome. And it was a Gospel with power which changed men. There was power in my mother's prayers and in my father's preaching and in our lusty hymn-singing. When those Lubwa Christians sang the old chorus – 'There is power, power, wonderworking power in the blood of the Lamb' – they meant it. And they could point to members of their family, neighbours and

18

friends who had been brought to Jesus and freed from all the dark forces of evil and superstition which never seemed far from the surface of the old life. My father died when I was eight years of age and no one who was part of the great congregation who attended his funeral could doubt the reality of Eternity.

Colin Morris has written somewhere that the first twenty minutes of any speech I make is more like a sermon than a political oration. Whether he meant that comment as a compliment or a criticism I do not know, but it is true in the sense that my style must have been influenced by the passionate preaching I so often heard in my youth. It was this power of the Gospel which enabled humble, and often unlettered village men to stand in the pulpit of the old brick church at Lubwa and speak with tongues of fire. They had passion, real passion, a quality noticeably lacking in much modern preaching – which is more likely to consist of a bout of moralizing about world affairs or some agile juggling with intellectual propositions which chase each other's tails until the congregation is dizzy.

To be honest, I no longer find my parents' faith satisfying. There is nothing strange about that. After all, my world is more complex than the one they knew. I have travelled the globe, in the Far East, Asia, Europe and the Americas let alone Africa, and felt the impact of other cultures and religions. This rich experience has led me to question, reassess and add to my youthful beliefs. Nevertheless, I do not repudiate what my parents taught me about God. It is as much a part of me as the colour of my eyes or the texture of my skin. Indeed, it never ceases to amaze me how, in moments of crisis, I revert instinctively to the passionate simplicity

of the old religion. When the crunch comes, it is
often the trustful prayers of my childhood I find upon
my lips. And even now, I have only to hear some of
those old hymns of my Lubwa days and tears spring to
my eyes. Let sophisticates sneer at such sentimentality.
It is something much deeper – a turning in on my
roots; the desire to share the certainty and assurance of
those village Christians – the hope against hope that the
God they never doubted will not let me down either
in my hour of need.

So now you understand why I insist on family
prayers, Grace at table and, whenever possible, the
daily reading together of the Bible. I am well aware of
a certain degree of silent rebelliousness amongst you.
And I also know that there is a school of thought
which deplores the forcing of a parent's religion down
his children's throats. 'Let children make up their own
minds about religion', say such experts. That seems to
me utter rubbish. Ought we to allow children to make
up their minds whether they will steal or be honest, tell
the truth or become habitual liars? Do we allow them
to decide whether they will learn to read and write? It
is for parents to pass on to children the fruits of their
experience, and if God is the most important reality in a
parent's life, then he has a duty to explain to his
children why this is so and what it has all meant to him.

Further, I am convinced that the spiritual dimension
is an integral part of the human personality. If it is not
developed, it does not disappear but becomes warped
and degenerate. And this can be just as destructive in
later life as a deformed moral sense. Of course I am
opposed to that type of religious teaching which is an
insult to the child's intelligence – the parrot-like

20

repetition of propositions about God which the developing mind will easily and rightly demolish, resulting in
bewilderment or cynicism. I personally believe that
it is the child's sense of mystery which has to be
encouraged. This is the heart of all true religion.
The teaching and all the rest of it is secondary – not
unimportant but secondary. Possibly the single most
important distinction the human mind must learn to
make is that between the unknown and the unknowable. The advance of learning will reduce the area of
the unknown, given time, but the unknowable is forever beyond its scope – it is that element of mystery at
the heart of everything, from simple objects like a
blade of grass to profound realities such as sacrificial
love.

If, when you are mature, you wish to reject what
I have taught you about God, so be it. But I am
determined that it is *good* religion that you may turn
your backs on: the best I am capable of teaching you.
There is no more moral choice involved in rejecting *bad*
religion than bad music or art. That is a matter of
taste, not of moral choice. But to come to the con-
clusion that God does not exist; that the great religions
have for thousands of years been perpetuating a fantasy
– *that* requires a truly heroic decision, for atheism is
not without its difficulties and hardships. Meanwhile,
we shall continue to explore the Faith together. They
say that if you learn to swim when a child and then fall
into a river twenty years later, the strokes will come
back to you instinctively. It is in this light I see the
teaching of religion to children. So that if you feel the
need of God in later life, you will have some idea where
to look for him. Believe me, there are many things

children find a drag and a bore and would gladly abandon, but it is very difficult in later life trying to regain that early lost ground.

I ought to add just a word about the relationship between religion and Zambian Humanism. What form that Humanism will take as the years wear on, I cannot know. I certainly do not regard myself as a philosopher permanently enriching the world's thought systems, but rather as a practical man confronted with a serious challenge and feeling my way towards a response. Historically in the West, Humanism has been an alternative to the supernatural interpretation of life. Western humanists, confident in the power and truth of science, rejected theistic religion, putting Man in God's place as the ultimate reality. That was a brave thing to do, but it is far removed from my understanding of Humanism which asserts the value of Man without attempting to clothe him in Divine attributes. My problem was this. Zambia is a country of many religions – Christianity, Judaism, Animism, Hinduism and Islam, and others. I did not feel it was my place as President of the new Republic to adjudicate between them, to declare this religion or that 'official' so far as the State is concerned. Each has the right to exist, and it is my desire that believers of all faiths should live together in harmony. We are, after all, human beings. We certainly cannot afford to add religious divisions to the tribal differences which threaten our national unity. There is surely nothing more unedifying than watching devotees batter unbelievers into submission in the name of the only true God! Because I happen to be one of those odd people who feels equally at home in a cathedral, synagogue, temple or mosque, I recognize the power inherent in all the major faiths and urgently desire to see that power harnessed for the welfare and good of humanity. Thus far, thank God, we have succeeded in Zambia in avoiding the undesirable alternatives: religious contention and strife on the one hand, and on the other the creation of some drab compromise which would lead to the loss of the distinctive character of this rich variety of faiths. There are many points of difference, even among the main religions represented in our own country, which seem at this moment in history to be irreconcilable, but there ought surely to be common ground in a high view of Man as the paramount creation of the Supreme Being.

So Zambian Humanism which makes the welfare of Man the central aim of national policy invites all religious believers to harness the power inherent in their faith for socially desirable ends. Humanism is neither antireligious, nor some superreligion. It is only 'anti' that kind of piety in a vacuum which devalues God's world by rendering the pious unavailable for the service of their fellowmen. Humanism operates on the boundary between religion and politics as a channel for the best gifts of all true faith: compassion, service, and love – to be lavished on the nation's people.

I take with the utmost seriousness, the power of every great religion to inspire in its followers the highest human qualities. Our nation badly needs such qualities, which are not necessarily inherent in any political philosophy, even nationalism. Only public servants and private citizens who demonstrate industriousness, integrity, service and compassion, can help to give the impersonal State a human face. So Zambian

Humanism is a challenge to all religious believers to live up to their claims and put their spiritual power at the service of their neighbours. Every gospel which speaks good news about God's care for his children has power. The tragedy is that so few religious believers seem to know it. Like children playing with sticks of dynamite; they have little idea of the power in their hands. Too much in church life reminds me of a great engine pounding away but driving nothing.

However you decide to answer the fundamental questions raised by religion, I hope you will come to appreciate that spiritual power locked up in every personality which can be released by faith. Don't, I beg of you, play around with religion. Reject the existence of God or else make him the centre of your lives but don't give him a brief and casual nod every Sunday. It is better to have a modest faith which is fully used than make grand protestations which are never heard beyond the doors of the church.

Education and Humanism

I discovered the power of knowledge at an early age, possibly because education at that time was a rare privilege rather than a universal right. Not only were schools few and widely scattered in colonial days, but education cost the princely sum of two shillings and sixpence a year – barely more than the price of a bottle of beer at the present time – but how many children of promise and intelligence were doomed to wasted lives because that single coin was beyond their parents' means? Even now I burn with anger when I remember friends of my boyhood whom poverty incapacitated in the struggle for achievement. I was fortunate to have been born at a Christian Mission with a primary school and a Teacher Training Institute. I was even luckier to be one of twenty-nine boys from all over the country chosen to be the initial intake at Munali Secondary School. The year was 1941. The West was in the throes of a great war during which countless thousands of young men educated beyond our wildest dreams were senselessly obliterated. But in our country, twenty-nine boys were being accorded the privilege of a higher education. Though the colonial authorities did not know it, they were virtually choosing the cabinet of the government of an independent Zambia. We privileged few never forgot the masses who did not share our good fortune and, in a sense, all the hundreds of millions of kwachas we have spent on schools, colleges and the University of Zambia since Independence have been an act of reparation for those lost years of colonialism. One of the inglorious monuments to the colonial era was a great scrap-heap of untapped human resource, on which might well have been inscribed some words of Alexander Pope:

Thus let me live unseen, unknown,
Thus unlamented let me die,
Steal from the world, and not a stone,
Tell where I lie.

It has taken the world a long time to realize that the true wealth of any nation resides in the trained minds of its people. After countless ages extravagantly wasteful of human talent, the day has at last dawned when

educated men and women are in great demand. Among
all the great changes which our century has seen, this
change of attitude towards education may well prove to
be the most profound in the long run. It is not too
much to say that any nation or people which does not
value trained intelligence is doomed.

But I confess to a great misgiving as I watch the
ceaseless stream of young men and women pour out of
our educational establishments clutching their degrees,
diplomas and certificates. Certainly we need all the
doctors, engineers, lawyers, teachers we can produce,
and even now must fill the gaps with expatriates who
come to Zambia as our guests to help us out temporarily. What worries me is that we seem to take a
functional view of education, regarding its products as
job fodder, to be fitted into some vocational slot as
they emerge from the machine. True education ought to
do more than equip people to earn a living. In particular, I hope we do not turn out a generation of one-
subject specialists who are almost illiterate if they step
one inch outside their field.

Many of our nation's problems are technical, and our
educational system is well on the way to producing the
talent which can solve them. But more abstract yet more
fundamental questions need to be answered, concerned
with where our country is going, what its goals are
and how we can attain them. We require more than
mere competence down the mine, at the office, in the
workshop, law court or operating theatre. What about
those other skills such as depth of judgment, a sense of
perspective and a compassionate understanding of
human motivation? Some people say that such qualities
are the hard won fruits of experience alone. I would be

the last to deny the importance of learning the lessons of experience but I do insist that the foundations of these humane skills can be laid in an educational system which never loses sight of the truth that it is a *person* and not just a brain that is being trained.

To highlight our problem from a different angle: what about those young people whose bent is towards art or music or theology? Some of our stern pragmatists regard such students as parasites because their work may contribute little to our gross national product. Yet who can doubt that these skills have a decisive effect upon the quality of our nation's life? I dread the thought of a country which is like a great ant-hill, with workers scurrying busily to and fro, efficient and industrious but without the capacity to enjoy life for its own sake.

I do not pretend to be an expert in educational theory, but as the one who has been elected by the people to lead our nation through the perilous days of its early life, I cannot avoid asking myself what all our frenzied educational activity is *for*? My Cabinet colleagues and myself must have in our minds some working definition of education if only because the greater part of our national budget is spent on it. I believe Zambian Humanism offers us a valuable clue.

Central to my understanding of Humanism is the striving towards an ideal of individual fulfilment. I want every member of our society to be given the chance to achieve the best that is in him or her. That is not just a pious cliché; it has vital social and political implications. Personal frustration is the chief source of social breakdown and political instability. People with powerful inner drives that find no constructive outlet are not just wasted national resources, they are also potentially destructive elements within society. Their pain distorts their judgment and like a wounded animal they attack blindly. So personal fulfilment must be the basis of a happy, peaceful and civilized society.

A society's educational system is the chief instrument it has devised to further the ideal of individual fulfilment. So our thinking about the aims of education must have reach and perspective and expand beyond the narrow frontiers of job expectation or mere career success. Our educators must address themselves to the larger task of stimulating the individual's emotional, spiritual and moral growth as well as his intellectual capacity. This large view of education takes the whole subject out of the exclusive sphere of the teacher and lays it as a burden on society as a whole, starting with the family and ending with the Legislative Assembly. When we have trained a child's mind we have done little more than make a few scratches on the surface of his personality, under which lie deep layers of thought and action. Vitality, creativeness and adaptability – these qualities which are both good in themselves and of great social value must be the fruit of a genuine educational process.

It used to be accepted that there should be a strong moral element in education. This is an important principle which should be maintained and where necessary reinforced. When I talk of a person fulfilling his potentialities I must add the qualification that the moral value of those potentialities is to be taken into account. Learning for learning's sake is not enough. Criminals learn cunning, slaves submissiveness and tyrants the arrogance of power. It is possible to learn

28

things which warp our judgment, constrict our vision and bring harm on ourselves, our families and our fellowmen. The fulfilment we seek through education must be within the framework of moral values which characterize Man at his best. Because our society has to be marshalled, almost regimented, to do the things necessary for our survival; because it is of the nature of the modern world to throw up vast organizations and generate social forces that dwarf the individual, for these reasons education ought to help people to defend themselves against whatever tends to depersonalization. I have no desire to preside over a nation of mindless puppets who jerk and jump when the strings are pulled. *Zambia Shall Be Free* was the title I gave to the autobiographical sketch I wrote at the height of our struggle for independence; that is not just the name of a book but a slogan which expresses my prayer and hope and determination to do what I can to help bring into existence a nation of free and responsible people who respond willingly to the challenge of desperate necessity.

This qualification must be added: we can neither applaud nor tolerate irresponsible and wholly selfish individual development. Freedom without moral commitment is aimless and self-destructive. Here is a tension of opposites which every educationalist must appreciate and try to harmonize – to instil in his students both a vigorous sense of individuality and at the same time a sense of shared purpose with their fellows.

Humanism is concerned with the individual both finding and losing himself. And this is not so contradictory as it sounds. The man I respect is the one who

29

has humbly placed himself at the service of a vision greater than himself, but who is able to give himself to a greater good because he has first achieved a mature individuality; who has not sacrified his unique personality to some corporate abstraction. It is this which distinguishes a disciplined society from a totalitarian State.

But ideals are one thing, achievements another. A long and difficult road lies ahead of our nation. In spite of all the efforts of Government and other agencies, I fear that many of our present generation of young people may never fulfil their potentialities. Their growth has been stunted by inherited evils it will take a long time to eradicate. A shanty town is hardly the setting in which personal fulfilment is likely to be fostered. The family trapped in poverty and ignorance can offer its children little stimulus other than a sense of bitter rebelliousness, of hate almost, that God, the Party, the Government, circumstance, or all four, have conspired to rob them of their rightful heritage. And hate, though a powerful driving force, can never lead to personal fulfilment because it sets up tensions within the person which tear him apart and often spill over into the community as a virulent poison. It is a national scandal that so many of our young people fail to realize their potentialities. It weighs on my own conscience and I hope on the conscience of our nation. At a time when our country has so many claims on its human resources, it is unthinkable that we should resign ourselves to a situation of wasted talent and energy either because educational opportunities are not available or because the products of our educational system cannot find creative openings for their gifts. A nation of matriculated road-sweepers has little on which to congratulate itself.

Any effective attack on this problem must be mounted on a wider front than our formal educational institutions. It must involve not only the school but also the home, the Church, the Party – and the hospital or clinic, for we must not forget the part that endemic diseases such as malaria and bilharzia as well as inadequate or unbalanced diet play in stunting human growth.

But it is not only in childhood and youth that obstacles to individual fulfilment abound. People like myself who are required to speak at university graduation ceremonies and school prize days are much given to claiming that education is a lifelong process. No young person with a grain of common sense needs to be told this, and yet we older people go on saying it; and this, not because it is the appropriate cliché for the occasion but because it is a truth that experience has taught us. How many mistakes we have made that cannot now be repaired! How many crossroads we have passed which are now behind us forever! My children, I beg of you, do not shut your minds when you leave school or university, as though you have accumulated enough knowledge to get you through the rest of your lives. If your schooling is successful, it will have taught you how to use your minds. The question remains: what will you use your minds *on*?

I am not, of course, claiming that the learning process continues uniformly through life. If that were so age and wisdom would be synonymous – and there are plenty of old fools around to disprove such a proposition! The sad truth, however, is that for many

C

people the learning process comes to an end so early that society abounds in freaks – adolescent minds in mature bodies. Obviously there *are* differences in the capacity of people to go on learning, but these differences must not be confused with differences in the degree of success achieved by individuals. There are those whom the world has rejected as unsuccessful who have had the private compensation of continuing to learn all their lives: there are prominent people in every society, widely hailed as successes, who stopped learning decades ago. They found a formula for wealth or fame at some point in their lives and continue to repeat it.

There is another side to this question of young people being denied the prospect of true fulfilment by hereditary or environmental factors outside their control. My own experience has been that a reasonable degree of hardship can help strengthen the bones and feed the tissues of resolve. Pasteur, the man who overcame a grievous physical handicap to discover immunization, said that fortune favours the prepared mind. I think fortune too, favours the determined will. There is in most people an inner drive, a seeking and exploring element in their character which either grows or withers away as they meet the various experiences of life. True education will foster this inner dynamic, without which our minds become dull and our imaginations stunted.

Now you know why I have hammered away again and again and in all my speeches on the theme of Humanism whatever my audience – farmers or civil servants, intellectuals or peasants, teachers or pupils, politicians or electorate. We cannot afford to consign this broad conception of education to a category separate from the main business of life nor to confine it to those between the ages of six and sixteen. Somehow we have to engage the whole nation in the task of securing individual fulfilment within the framework of moral purpose.

The years that have followed Zambia's independence have seen a dramatic expansion in our programmes of adult education so that those who never had schooling as children can get it, and those who have been educated continue their studies. But this is not enough. Every one of the media which touch the minds of our people must be harnessed to this great cause. It makes nonsense, for example, in a developing nation such as ours, to regard radio and television merely as channels of entertainment; means of escape to some colourful dreamland from the harsh realities of the deprived life. I am appalled by the canned rubbish we project by the hour on our television screens. We talk of such trivia as entertainment, but it is more: it is a form of education, but a debilitating and bad one. Our people are learning by what they hear on the radio and see on the television screen, but they are often learning the wrong things – the values of materialism, the elevation of crime and cupidity, the glorification of characters who contribute nothing to society except the example of easy morals and luxurious living.

There is deadly danger in these forms of communication when an unsophisticated people are exposed to them before they have had the time and opportunity to develop the faculty of discrimination. The sheer marvel of the medium itself invests what is transmitted through it with a spurious but nonetheless powerful authority.

People *believe* because they have heard or seen it on radio or television. We have got to do a lot more hard thinking about the role and place of the media of communication in our national life. Too rigorous governmental control can lay us open to the charge of brain-washing or propaganda-mongering. Nevertheless, I do not take the view that commitment to freedom demands an anarchy of ideas, magnified and amplified to the point where our democratically chosen national philosophy is undermined.

And we must cast our net even wider than the media of communication. Unions, party branches, church congregations, professional organizations and social clubs can all make an important contribution to individual growth and learning if they get their priorities right and recognize their strategic importance. There are many opportunities open to the employer, for example, who is willing to acknowledge his responsibility for furthering the education as well as developing the skills of those who work for him. And let it not be forgotten that the Zambian Government is our country's largest employer. The example must begin here. As I travel about the country I have been delighted to find Government departments giving civil servants of all grades the opportunity of studying together and discussing literature about Humanism which our Ministry of National Guidance has produced.

A long time ago, our United National Independence Party adopted the slogan 'Each One Teach One' as a way of engaging everyone in the task of nation-building and of supplementing our formal education system. Pompous though it may sound, this multiplicity of effort has as its goal the creation of a great nation by

fostering individual growth at every age, in every walk
of life and in every conceivable way. Only by so doing
can we keep faith with those who fought and sacrificed
to obtain independence. No nation born out of fire and
struggle has the right to choose a trivial destiny, a
second-rate existence.

Once our concern for individual fulfilment becomes
a national preoccupation, our formal education system
will be faced with a challenge beyond anything they
have yet experienced. I have claimed that much
depends upon the individual's attitude towards learning,
his responsibility to bring to full flower whatever gifts
God has given him. This defines the task of our schools
and colleges. They must excite the minds of their
students and strengthen their wills for the task of
constant self-examination and reshaping. We cannot be
content with the old system of stuffing students like
sausages or training them like performing animals. Our
teachers must have a sense of vocation which leads
them to regard themselves as much more than salary-
earning technicians. We are entrusting them with our
nation's future. If they fail then in a generation or so
we shall be saddled with a half-educated society doomed
to the self-destroying values of materialism. The
teacher must take education beyond the mechanical
stage of packing the student's mind with information.
He has to be given the equipment to judge, to assess,
to process for himself the ideas presented to him.
Above all, he must learn to distinguish between the
shoddy and worthwhile, the permanently enriching and
the shortlived, the noble and the secondrate.

I see education in this way: the teacher shapes the
tools, life provides the material, but what is wrought

depends on the individual himself. If we can accept
without reservation the implications of our humanistic
belief in individual fulfilment, and if we can get enough
of our leaders to catch something of the vision, then
we shall have enshrined a highly significant purpose at
the heart of the nation's life and lifted all education to a
new level of meaning. We shall have committed ourselves to transforming all the institutions of our
society – truly a revolution in which not a drop of
blood has been spilt!

I have a sneaking feeling that my philosophizing
about education may have bored those of you whose
bent is towards the more practical or physically active
aspects of life; who regard classroom work as a restful
interlude between bouts on the football or hockey field
(as I did myself once upon a time). But I beg of you,
do not miss my main point, which is aimed at each of
you personally. I covet for you the best education you
are mentally capable of sustaining. And I hope that
your education will enable you to achieve overall
harmony in your lives – intellectual development within
a framework of strong moral values, aimed not merely
at job-success but social usefulness. May you know
that peace of mind which comes of realizing that you
have wasted nothing, regret nothing and repudiate
nothing which can add to your stature as human
beings.

Someone has said that education is the pursuit of
excellence. Well, I wouldn't quarrel with that. Don't
accept second-best as an acceptable standard for
yourselves; don't lower your goals; don't slide into
compromises in the interests of a comfortable, not too-
taxing existence. No one will be prouder than your

father if you attain excellence, either to a great or modest degree. The context is unimportant. It is better to be an excellent housewife rather than a mediocre doctor, an excellent parent rather than an incompetent Cabinet minister, an excellent carpenter rather than a successful but crooked business man.

Do you get my point?

Standards and values

Writing this to you seems to have stimulated my brain cells. I want to take a little further this idea of excellence because it is a one-word description of what lies behind my own personal pilgrimage as a human being.

A society which does not believe in anything will never achieve excellence. What do we Zambians believe in? And how passionately do we feel about those values and standards we are pledged to uphold in our Constitution? This is a timely question. These words are being written on the eve of the eighth Anniversary of Independence. It is a time for stock-taking, for reassessment of priorities, for striking a trial-balance of the books of national account to see what stands to our credit and which of our enterprises have failed.

I have already discussed at length the theme which above all else I passionately believe in – the importance of the individual and his fulfilment. This is no recently acquired conviction. As all my family knows, it is now over twenty years since I last ate meat. I can still see clearly in my mind that day when I watched a group of poor African women being manhandled outside a white-owned butcher's shop because they were protesting

37

against the quality and price of the rotten meat he was trying to foist off on them. I swore then never to eat anything my poorest fellow-Africans could not afford. That form of protest seemed to many at the time melodramatic and even now somewhat eccentric, but whenever I sit down for a meal and refuse the meat course it is a useful reminder to me that the welfare of the individual means the poorest, least-regarded, easiest ignored of all God's children, or it means nothing.

But here lies a problem that you will have to wrestle with as I have done. Concern for the individual is not enough. What about the welfare of society too? Personal fulfilment on a wide scale can only occur in a society designed to cherish the individual, and with strength to protect him, especially if he should be one of those too weak to protect himself. Such a society does not just appear by chance like a four-leafed clover. It is the end-product of the concern of free and enlightened men who are prepared to accept responsibilities beyond those of their private preoccupations. The truly free man can live for himself only by living for his society. And a free society will not survive or deserve to survive if the tradition of individual fulfilment decays from within. It is also true that free men can exist only in a free society – an obvious but easily forgotten truth.

The founding fathers of our nation were well aware how vulnerable our country was, living on the fringes of great power struggles, still unresolved, to determine the shape of Southern Africa. Our first aim had to be to prove that we were capable and worthy of survival as a free society, making good our promises and maintaining the values which inspired the freedom

movement. More than this, we had to prove our
vigour, our capacity to achieve excellence. For who,
with any legitimate pride, wishes to lead a mediocre
nation, ambling along, eking out a ramshackle sort of
existence. I want Zambia to *count*, not in military terms
or even in the world of international finance but as a
nation of which no citizen of goodwill and dedication
need be ashamed – a nation constantly engaged in
enlarging the frontiers of freedom for its ordinary
people.

There is no shortage of prophets of doom who claim
that the free society is an illusion in such a world as
ours; that the aggression, sloth and self-indulgence of
human nature must be curbed by ruthlessly applied
social and political controls. Of course there is some
truth in this view, and any leader who acted on the
assumption that he was presiding over a colony of
angels would get a rude shock. But one need not be a
starry-eyed idealist to reject the view that Man's nature
is immovably fixed at the level of his lowest instincts;
that men together can strive not merely for survival
but for excellence.

On the anniversary of our Independence I ask myself
whether our people are demonstrating a spirit of
national dedication or sliding down the greasy path of
self-aggrandizement. I know that some of the most
prominent members of our society have said in effect
'Let the nation go to hell so long as my own interests
flourish and my bank balance grows!' It is because I
detect such attitudes amongst my fellow-citizens that I
have grave misgivings about our future. Yet I also
know that once upon a time, and not so very long ago
at that, our people accepted hardship and suffering to

39

achieve independence. We invested too much blood and life in our struggle for freedom to let it slip away by inches now.

Possibly I am an incurable optimist, but I still have enough faith in my fellow-Zambians to believe that they will respond to a ringing call for moral commitment and an end to the apathy and cynicism which hover like a cloud over the nation. By the time the youngest of you can understand what I now write, you will also be able to judge whether my faith was well founded. Through my dedication to Humanism, I have made my appeal to the idealism of my fellow men rather than to their baser instincts. If I should be proved wrong, then it is better that I go back to my village and leave the business of guiding this nation to others who have a more calculating view of human nature.

I hope I have not given the impression that I regard national dedication as a grim and drab business, all clenched teeth and sweat. It is my earnest desire to serve a *happy* people. You will, I hope, discover, later in life that it is not an invariable rule that one must be miserable in order to be good. Happiness can be a powerful motive force towards excellence provided it is not confused with ease, tranquillity or the cessation of effort. It is easy to be satisfied if one's hopes are modest and one's aims easily attainable. The truth is that happiness as the sense of total gratification is an animal rather than human state, appropriate to birds or oxen but not to men.

Most rational people want meaning in their lives, the feeling that the various elements in their personalities do not neutralize each other but can be aligned to some

overall purpose. When we strive for excellence we are
enrolling ourselves in an ancient and honourable cause –
the agelong struggle of some men to improve the
quality of life for all mankind. Man struggling rest-
lessly for excellence in his chosen field has achieved
most of what is worthwhile in history. The nineteenth-
century writer Hazlitt wrote: 'Man is the only animal
that laughs and weeps; for he is the only animal that is
struck by the difference between what things are and
what they ought to be.' If you are unaware of that gulf
or have little interest in bridging it, then you will find
that by some inexorable law, 'things as they are' will
get worse, the gap will grow wider and yet one more
civilization will sink into decline and eventual oblivion.

My experience has been that men who are happy to
settle for poor performance, easy attainment and
well-trodden paths become dictator-fodder; the root
cause of war; the upholders, through sheer apathy, of
every human vice and oppression.

The years ahead promise to be difficult and dangerous. We shall need to marshall all our wisdom, our
talent and vitality, to preserve in existence a free society
– a society worth living in and suffering for. Social
virtue has this in common with a human limb: if it is not
exercised regularly its owner loses the use of it. Long
continued incapacity to understand the need for
dedication and sacrifice can have only one outcome. We
shall lose the capacity to set for ourselves high goals
and struggle seriously to attain them. The only virtues
which flower in any society are those which that society
nourishes by conscious and continued effort. A people's
identity, especially when it lacks the long continuities
of historical development, as we do, is shaped by the

qualities and values they celebrate, recognize instantly and respect profoundly.

By comparison with the days of the freedom struggle, when our goal was simple and easily dramatized in the minds of the people, our developing nation seems so complex that ordinary men do not find it easy to identify with its goals. Technical questions of economic policy, worries about the price of copper, about the balance of payments and so on, seem so mysterious to the ordinary man that the power and will of the nation appears to be vested in a group of specialists rather than the mass of the people. It is an old cliché that politics is too important to be left to the politicians. By the same token, our nation's destiny cannot be assigned to a technological elite with their complex formulae and advanced theories. We certainly need the help of experts and are grateful for those who have offered us their services, but they can no more define and motivate the people towards our national goals than the constitutional lawyers we sometimes consulted could win our freedom for us. This problem is not unique to Zambia. Technocracy is a disease of all modern nations and it engenders in ordinary citizens the severest shock the human system can sustain – a numbing sense of uselessness.

What, then, can we do? Over and above all the facets of the problem of the ordinary citizen's identification with the aims of the nation, there is one simple challenge it is not beyond the individual to understand, however humble he may be. I return to it again and again in my speeches and writings. It is the appeal to every single citizen to recognize that if he wants a free society he must be worthy of it. He must foster the simple quality of integrity in all his dealings and instil it in his children. We need to get this message across by every means at our command. The people must be made to understand that a cynical community is a corrupt community. To use the word in its broadest sense, the nation must hear in ringing tones a gospel, preached in a thousand accents, in all our languages, by all who call themselves leaders, proclaiming shared aims which are attainable and durable.

Some of our critics say that we are uncertain what our shared aims are; that we are drifting because we've lost the common enemy of colonialism which united us in struggle. It is true that a people under stress are prone to look around for some common enemy, some scapegoat on whom to lay all their troubles. And when people cast around for mischief, they have little difficulty finding it. They discover common enemies in the most surprising places – in an outside country or another tribe or in Government itself.

I do not believe that our people will be fooled into thinking that there is any way forward in trying to concentrate understandable frustration on convenient targets which, because they are beyond our range, do not require any action towards amelioration. I do not think that the ordinary man, in his heart, is in any doubt about our shared aims as a nation. He knows what they are. He knows that they are difficult of achievement. And he knows that we have not achieved them.

Need I give any examples? We want a nation in which no one is denied the basic sinews of a truly human existence – a roof over his head, food in his belly, the opportunity to develop his talents, to go as far as his abilities will take him. We want freedom. We believe that no man was born to have someone else's foot on his neck, or someone else's hand over his mouth. We want every man to be respected, to be treated with dignity and justice. We want every citizen to have a say in the government that rules over him; a government that is responsive to his will, aware of his deficiencies and determined to correct them. We want Man to be established at the heart of our society for what he is in himself – not a political counter or an economic unit, not the plaything of the wealthy and powerful; not Man a walking stomach or a gaping mouth to swallow all the propaganda and lies that those of evil inclination feed to him, but Man, an eternal spirit, who cherishes in his heart all the values which can make our nation great.

I could extend the catalogue indefinitely, but there is no need to do so. We *know* what our aims ought to be, just as surely as we know that there is no short cut to their attainment. They are the universal goals of all rational men, enshrined in the literature, philosophy and religion of the ages. Courageous men and women of many races, cultures and centuries have spent life-times of frustration, endurance and effort in pursuit of them. Others have fought and died for them. But the fact that millions of men and women have died defending essential human values does not ensure the survival of those values unless others are prepared to live for them. Unlike the Pyramids, great monuments of the spirit cannot stand untended. They must be nourished in each generation by the allegiance of believing and dedicated men and women. Every free man, in his work and in his family life, in his public behaviour and in the

44

secret places of his heart, should see himself as a builder
and maintainer of the values of his society. Children
must be taught, as they have the capacity to understand,
how great a heritage it is that will one day be passed
on to them . . .

Just as I am trying now to light a flame in your
minds and inviting you to spend yourselves to help
make your country and your world a better place for
your own children to live in.

Communicating with other people

Let us leave serious topics for a while and deal with
some things of a more intimate, personal nature –
trivia in comparison to the great issues of nation-
building but precious to me because they helped to
make me who and what I am.

I want to impress on you the usefulness and even
necessity for learning to express yourselves clearly and
well. As a boy I was very shy and although I did not
find teaching from a textbook in front of me too difficult,
my first sallies in public speaking for what was then the
African National Congress in the Chinsali area were
purgatory! But it was during my political apprenticeship that I learned the power of words, well chosen,
carefully put together and clearly expressed. After all,
you can have a head so crammed full of brains that
you can't get your hat on but if you cannot express all
that knowledge, it may as well not be there; you have
no great advantage over the village idiot. The fact that
you, like me, use both an African vernacular and the
English language, poses some problems because the

45

two languages are constructed and articulated dif-
ferently. I hope you will never lose your mastery of
your mother tongue, but English is the language of
international communication, and so you must become
proficient in it. After all, words are power. In all that
I have written thus far, I am conscious that both
religion and education are communicated by means of
the spoken and written word. No matter how great the
truth, it is only as powerful as there are words by
which to transmit it.

If you study the life of any demagogue, it is clear
that the mastery of words is part of the secret of his
success. Words are used to articulate the desires and
frustrations of the people in vivid imagery and with
passionate conviction. In our own fight in Zambia
against the Federation of Rhodesia and Nyasaland and
for our independence, our main armament was not guns
but words – thousands and thousands of words, written
and spoken to rally our people, to lay our claims before
the British Government and the world, to express our
anger and frustration at the denial of our birthright to
rule our own country. Words are power. Inarticulateness
is impotence.

I do not for a moment imagine that all of you will
end up as politicians. But whatever career you choose,
make no mistake that the ability to express yourself
clearly will make all the difference to your success.
Moreover there is a glowing satisfaction in being able
to say or write precisely what you wish to express. I
suppose I make hundreds of speeches a year to bodies
as varied as the United Nations General Assembly and
a small group of villagers assembled under a tree in
some remote part of our country. But I struggle always

to refine my gift of expression, not merely because this is one aspect of individual fulfilment but also because imprecision can be the cause of confusion, uncertainty and even conflict. Take that one word 'Federation' – our country was almost plunged into civil war, and a racial war at that, because the word meant one thing to Africans and a very different thing to white negotiators. Where important matters of national policy are concerned, I cannot afford to be obscure or loose in expression. The sense of what one says must be so precise that it cannot be blurred or altered in transmission to become something quite different. What is said in Lusaka must be equally clear from Chadiza to Zambezi and from Livingstone to Mbala.

It is claimed that Africans are natural talkers, and it is true in the sense that conversation by the hour is still the main diversion in rural areas where there are no cinemas or television sets. But this is a skill which needs constant attention. I learn new words almost every day. I read and work with a dictionary close at hand so that when I come across an unfamiliar word I can check its meaning and add it to my vocabulary. I would advise you to do the same. Never allow your eye to light on an unknown word without taking the trouble to find out exactly what it means. And whenever you get the opportunity, listen to masters of the language; how they put words together and the cadences of their expression. The speeches of Winston Churchill for example are rich in arresting expressions; possibly a little too rich for these modern days – but Churchill was a master of the English language who by the passion of his oratory could inspire a whole people caught up in a terrible war to stand against

D

aggression. Another master of the art of communication was the Mahatma Gandhi. His writings repay careful study, not only because of their content but also the beautiful way in which he expressed himself. His language was as simple as his way of life; he knew what he wanted to say, and said it with economy and clarity.

Many generations of Africans all over the continent were introduced to the written word through the Bible, first in vernacular translation and then as their education improved, in the English version. Through the ages that book made millions literate before the right to a formal education was won by the masses. I myself have heard simple village Elders, unlettered men, speaking in the noble English of the time of King James, thanks to their study of the Bible. Those who attended your grandmother's funeral at Lubwa will never forget the powerful oration of Donald Siwale, who being over ninety years of age, was denied your educational opportunities yet expressed himself in faultless English style.

Read good books, and read more and more of them. Don't waste your time with poorly written printed trash. Better collect a small library of what are called classics – books you can read again and again with profit – rather than litter your shelves with books whose ideas are paltry and whose language is thin, so that to read them once is more than enough. When I was a poor teacher, my library consisted only of the Bible, a hymn book, Waldo Trine's *In Tune with the Infinite*, some of Gandhi's writings and as many of the novels of Dickens as I could afford. Not a very elaborate array, but each book was thumbed and worn with constant use. Poetry is a taste I developed rather

48

later. I have even tried my hand at writing a little! But reading poetry is one of the best ways of learning the 'music' of language – the flow of sentences, the weight of words in their most telling order, the vivid image conveyed in a line or so.

Learn to love words. It is an acquired taste, and will not come easily to some of you. But remember that the finest compliment you can pay any listener is to address him as clearly and carefully as you know how; just as there is no greater discourtesy to someone than to speak to him in slovenly, badly expressed phrases which indicate that you really do not care whether he understands or not. If you get the opportunity to speak in public, take it, even though your knees tremble and your mouth goes dry. There is no better way of developing self-confidence, and the discipline of public speaking is admirable, even though you have no intention of becoming either preacher or politician.

I ought to add one obvious warning. There is little point in learning how to speak clearly unless you have something to say! Talking for the sake of spinning a web of words is a futile activity; one, alas, not unknown in the profession of politics. A well stored mind is the essential prerequisite of the art of com-munication. Reading, listening, observing, are all means of gathering information – but this must be turned into ideas through reflection and mental exploration. Great ideas, well expressed, have changed the world. I hope you can make at least a tiny dent on affairs through using the gifts God has given you, plus the skills you learn for yourselves in this all-important business of communication.

Music

My other great love, besides that of words, is music, which has played a great and central role in my life. Africans are born, I think, with an innate sense of rhythm – the beat of the drums sends pulses through our systems and awakens deep emotions and strange feelings that link us to our ancestors from time immemorial. Christian hymns and African drums, sometimes both together, aroused in me an abiding love for music. It may surprise those of you who now regard me as a *Shikulu* – an old man – to learn that I once embarked upon a shortlived career as what was in those days called a 'crooner' with a school concert troupe called 'The Evening Birds'! Singing and playing the guitar is probably still my favourite hobby, though I am aware that the younger of you, accustomed to a more frantic beat regard me as something of a 'square'.

All people who have known sorrow and difficulty turn to music as solace, and I have been no exception. I have sung in jail to pass the time, and led the singing at great political rallies because there are certain lofty sentiments which are too precious or too elusive to express except through music. One could compile a musical history of the freedom struggle – songs of freedom that expressed our deepest hopes and longings and strengthened us to fight and fight again for our independence. There are some things which cannot be said but can be sung. The troubadours of old, serenading their ladies, found it possible to sing what they would be too shy or selfconscious to say. I am, I suppose, an emotional person, easily moved to tears or stirred to action by beautiful music, and I learned very early on that my shyness and selfconsciousness vanished as soon as I started plucking my guitar or struck up a hymn or political song. In some curious way, music also allays my fears. The Chinsali area used to be notoriously lion infested and some of my political trips in the early days of Congress involved miles of bicycle travel along lonely bush paths. I would sing my head off, no doubt frightening the life out of any curious lion, but certainly keeping my own courage up.

For me, a world without music is unthinkable, and a nation, however dynamic and economically advanced, which is too busy to make music, is just too busy, and that's all there is about it. Music is the gateway to a magic world: for me at least it has dissolved prison walls, healed emotional wounds and filled me with a sense of harmony and wellbeing when all about me was strife and contention. It is interesting that of all God's creatures, only man and the birds have been given the gift of music. The birds have melody but only man is capable of harmony. This is surely a parable of the ultimate harmony that is intended to bind all life together in one great unity, unbroken by war, oppression and vicious competition.

I think that Western observers who go on talking about the 'primitive' beat of the drums in Africa are perpetuating a fiction. Music, like poetry or great art, is a vehicle for appealing to the intellect of man by means of his senses. I find that I am at my most creative and reflective when my being has been suffused by beautiful music, and some of my old political comrades who know me well, were always ready to strike up a political song if they felt one of my speeches at a great rally was lagging a little. The song always put some spark and passion back into me!

Don't make the mistake of assuming that the music of a people is a kind of luxury to be indulged in if and when its social, political and economic needs have been met. Music is the soul of the nation. The musician, the dancer, the poet, are not peripheral to our national development. They are the best possible indicators of the extent to which we are achieving our noblest aims. They are the chroniclers of our history, the recorders of our triumphs; our solace in difficulty; our comfort in defeat; our protection against despair and disillusionment. You can't set a balance sheet to music, which is why the materialists are wrong when they claim that Man is economically determined and every other aspect of his life is secondary.

If it is true that the gift of musical performance is to some extent hereditary, then given the love of music of your mother and myself, there is a fair chance that some of you will achieve some competence in making music. But even if not, I hope you will acquire the art of listening to music. For that requires only the skills of patience and discipline. Of course, I cannot dictate what your interests in life shall be, but I am sure that without an appreciation of music your lives will be immeasurably poorer.

Quality and equality

Well, after that pleasant diversion, let's go back to my main theme. I have talked about the pursuit of excel-

lence as a worthwhile goal which is both individually
fulfilling and socially useful. But there is a tension here
which must be identified and, if possible, resolved.
Does the pursuit of excellence conflict with one of the
main drives of the modern democratic State – the
importance of equality? Can we be both equal and
excellent too? This is a vital question. On the one hand
we need those who can demonstrate excellence in many
fields of endeavour, on the other, the mass of the
people, quite rightly demand equality. To what extent
then dare we favour the excellent without creating an
aristocracy of talent – an elite which may form the basis
of a new kind of class division? I have given much
thought to this problem.

There is an old saying: 'You can't keep a good man
down!' Unfortunately, our bitter experience of
colonialism and racism has taught us that not only can
elitist societies keep a good man down but in some
cases they have kept a whole race down. So historically our first aim as a people has been to ensure
equality, and to oppose those systems which deny
basic human rights to any man because of factors
which are beyond his control, and about which he can
do nothing.

Take the system of *Apartheid* as practised to the South
of us. This ideology is in direct contradiction to
Humanism. They are two utterly contrary views of the
nature of Man. And there is no possibility, in the long
run of any compromise between them – what one
affirms, the other denies; what one seeks to build up,
the other tries to smash down; what one holds dear,
the other regards as worthless.

Apartheid is made up of three elements, each of

which strikes at the root of a different aspect of human equality:

1. *The right to be. Apartheid* denies this right by its use of stereotypes, false but highly emotive images of the Black race, demonstrated by the use of insulting names such as Nigger, Kaffir, Boy, Munt, each of which conjures up in the minds of those who use such epithets a perverted and cruel image of the one so described. The philosophy of *Apartheid* denies to Black people the right to *be*; it forces them to conform to an image which the so-called Master Race has created of them to prove Black inferiority and White superiority.

This philosophy of Black inferiority is enshrined in the laws and customs of South Africa and denies the right of Black people to be themselves – themselves not as another race sees them but as God made them. This is the terrible sin of robbing a people of their future. They are fixed, frozen as it were, in a given point of time. There can be no development of personality, no room for spiritual attainment, for either excellence or equality; no better tomorrow. As in an enormous block of ice, the Black people are immobile. Whereas a White child has the potential for excellence, to achieve great things in any profession, walk of life, sport or job; whereas he has, in theory, limitless development, the Black child can only be what his fathers were. He is consigned to primitive darkness, imprisoned within a system which hampers his movements, confines his energies and cripples his spirit. He must remain forever a Kaffir or a Nigger or a Boy. He can only be what a group of White men, holding political power at a particular point in history decree he *must* be. And this image, upon which exponents of *Apartheid* base their government policies, systems of education and economic doctrines, their religion even, is made up of a snake's nest of myths about the Black man's past and fears of his future. Those who preach *Apartheid* are guilty of breaking the second commandment, in which God forbids the making of graven images. These wicked men, who boast of their godliness, have created a graven image of the Black man, not to worship but to denigrate and sneer at.

Humanism, on the other hand, believes that God has given to every man, regardless of his ethnic origins, an open future – the power to become what he might be – the guarantee of equality; the possibility of excellence. It recognizes that there is an element of the mysterious, the as yet undeveloped, in every personality, and so denies the right of anybody to make images of another race which must imprison and pervert this mysterious power.

Whereas *Apartheid* declares the degradation of some men, Humanism affirms the glory of all men. There is nothing sentimental about the Humanist's view of Man. Both his experience and his insight into his own nature teach that the equality of men is a matter of value, not ability; some men have gifts which are denied to others, but all men are capable of far greater achievements than they have so far shown, and the social and political system must be so organized as to allow every man to reach the limit of his possibilities, great or modest. *Apartheid* forces *some* men to live at a level far below their best. Humanism seeks to evoke from *all* men a response better than their best – to increase the sum of human power and fulfilment.

2. *The right to belong. Apartheid* denies this right

through its policy of segregation of races. It imposes unnatural divisions on society, choosing a totally irrelevant standard, that of skin pigmentation, to determine the boundaries of community. The so-called doctrine of Separate Development creates a social monster in just the same way that robbing a child of all contact with his parents and friends will turn him into an individual monstrosity. So South Africa's policy of segregation is aimed at building two nations – one of supermen and the other of submen. This is morally indefensible, economic lunacy and politically explosive. It is morally indefensible because God created man in His own image, and only the totality of human community can demonstrate the fullness of the divine image. Segregated groups cannot demonstrate this image of God; they transform it into horrible caricatures – of the Devil in the case of those who gather themselves together on the basis of some fancied superiority, and of the Animal, in the case of those who are herded together because of some false inferiority.

Apartheid is economic lunacy because modern economic systems depend not only on the maximum use of human resources but also on the application of these resources at the point of their greatest effectiveness. Hence men who could increase the economic performance of the nation are allowed to rot in reserves and Bantusans far distant from the places where they could make the maximum contribution to the nation's economic life. Lastly, segregation is a politically explosive concept which those international businessmen at present scurrying to invest in South Africa would do well to ponder. By definition, segregation implies unequal distribution of resources and enshrines injustice. It gives a monopoly of wealth to one group and keeps the other in penury. By its gross deformity of the shape of true community it generates tension which must sooner or later blow the whole nation apart if genuine indignation can find no constitutional outlet. And in a modern world, shrunk in size because of the universality of communication and networks of power, any situation of chronic injustice must sooner or later engulf the great powers and produce a holocaust which could lead to world war.

The Humanist believes that men belong to each other; that no man is an island, self-entire. His estimate of Man is based on the assumption that no race or class or group has a monopoly of all human gifts and powers. Each natural group has certain weaknesses which need the reinforcement of the strength of others, and it is through human interaction that Man achieves his potential. Segregation denies the richness and variety of the human heritage. It proposes the monotony of a garden filled with flowers of a single colour, the loneliness of a community of only one sex, or the impotence of a body comprising only a single organ.

For the Humanist the fundamental human right is the right to love and to be loved. Segregation, on the other hand, generates hate because it strengthens fear of the unknown, and it is a truth of human nature that we tend to hate rather than love that which we fear through ignorance.

Of course there is such a thing as natural human community, but the basis on which individuals come together in groups has nothing to do with such artificial similarities as skin colour, but rather with the drive of people with a common history to achieve a

common destiny. Increasingly in the modern world,
even the nation-state is being found defective as a
vehicle of human destiny and the first slender filaments
of world community are being woven between men
everywhere. Humanism, therefore, harnesses the power
of historical destiny, whilst *Apartheid* is fighting against
history, and it is a matter of record that those nations
which have attempted to resist history have been swept
aside.

3. *The right to have. Apartheid* denies this right by its
belief in discrimination. The Charter of the United
Nations Organization sets out certain fundamental
rights which all men possess for no other reason than
that they are human. It is the willingness of any nation
to grant these rights to every one of its citizens without
regard to their colour or class or ability which marks
it out as just and good. *Apartheid* reserves certain
rights to those of a particular racial group – education,
job possibilities, the power to vote and to have a share
in government, even the right to worship God freely.
Others have these rights either entirely withheld or
granted only in limited degree. For the Apostle of
Apartheid, it is one race which is the Messianic Race,
apparently chosen by God to lord it over all others.
In both cases, these beliefs are unbiblical and erroneous.
God's dealings are with all men equally and the only
messianic group consists of the ones chosen from
every race and language and colour who acknowledge
his Lordship. Just as all men are sinners, so all men
have the right to redemption, and by virtue of that right
are entitled to all other rights which the State has the
power to bestow. For the State is a God-given instrument for the earthly protection of Man's immortal soul.

One must note a vitally important distinction between *Apartheid* and any political ideology. For it is clear to every thinking person that one can change one's beliefs whether they be religious, political, cultural or anything else. But, of course, God is the only one who decides what the skin pigmentation of a man shall be. In other words, a human being is free to choose his ideology, but it is God who makes us what we are in terms of colour.

Humanism operates in the belief that the only discrimination allowed by God is that in favour of those who without the protection of the State would be at the mercy of superior power. So whereas *Apartheid* discriminates in favour of the strong, the wealthy and the powerful, Humanism discriminates in favour of the weak and underprivileged. It recognizes that a society of equality is a dream until all men can engage in healthy competition from a position of equal opportunities. Every man, woman and child has an equal right to a place at the feast of life, and to make this possible, the main policy drive of any humanist nation must be to reduce those inequalities which rob men of their chances through no fault of their own.

To sum up: what is at stake in Southern Africa underneath all the arguments about supply of arms, economic sanctions, etc. is simply Man's right to be truly human. *Apartheid* maintains that a man's role in society is ascribed – by law and custom and history – and cannot be changed. Humanism believes that a man's role in society is achieved and that it is the duty of the State to do everything possible to strengthen human weakness, curb human greed, and provide every possible facility to enable its citizens to expand their horizons and release the God-given abilities locked up within them.

It was necessary for me to analyse *Apartheid* not only to explain the basis of our quarrel as Humanists with governments that practise it but also to show how deepseated our belief in fundamental human equality really is. Yet equality is easier to toss about as a catch-word than to define with any precision. Everyone in a free country believes in it but many are confused on the subject. We can get general agreement on broad principles that are almost clichés through constant usage, but to make equality the basis of national policy is much more difficult. We believe that in the final matters of life and death, all men are equally worthy of our concern and care. We come as equals into the world and as equals we go out of it. Beyond this we believe all men equal in the possession of certain legal, civil and political rights. It was Aristotle, I believe, who claimed that the only stable State is one in which all men are equal before the law.

But experience teaches us that men are not equal in their native gifts nor in their motivations; and it follows that they will not be equal in their achievements. That is why equality of opportunity has assumed such a central role in the democratic philosophy. Even then, equality of opportunity is by no means as simple as it sounds. In practice, it means an equal chance to compete within the framework of goals and the structure of rules established by a particular society; and this tends to favour certain people with certain kinds of gifts. Zambian society, for example, may ensure for each of you equality of opportunity with every other child. But it can only place before all children the range

60

of opportunities available in this particular society. If you have an undiscovered talent for chariot racing or writing a beautiful script on an illuminated parchment, then you have missed your century! You have been born later than your time. That is unavoidable. But it is proper to recognize that even if a society achieved perfect equality of all opportunity, it would still inevitably favour those whose gifts fit the requirements of that society.

Even though we have done much in Zambia as a matter of national policy to pursue the ideal of equality, we are still far from attaining it. Where there are differences in culture and background as great as those which exist as between Whites and Blacks, rural areas and towns, businessmen and peasants, even free schooling may not compensate for the tremendous variations in opportunity represented by dramatically different home backgrounds. We cannot rest easy in the face of such inequality of circumstance, but short of regimenting the nation and intolerably interfering with the private lives of citizens, even to the extent of telling them what they will earn and how they will spend their salaries, we cannot equalize life standards.

There is a certain extreme egalitarianism in some parts of the world which militates against the attainment of excellence. People of special gifts, unusually great endowments, far from being valued, are thought to be more trouble to society than they are worth. Hence there is always a danger that too rigorous a view of egalitarianism can degenerate into the glorification of mediocrity. It was the Danish philosopher Kierkegaard who warned against the danger of an egalitarianism so extreme as to be 'unrelieved by the smallest eminence'.

It is not easy for passionate believers in democracy

61

like ourselves to dwell on the differences in capacity between men. Democratic philosophy tends to ignore such differences where possible, and to belittle them where it could not ignore them. And it has had some warrant for this stringent view. The enemies of democracy have often quoted the unequal capacities of men as an excuse to persecute or even wipe out whole groups thought to be inferior. One only has to study the history of Nazi Germany with its deeply held belief that the Aryan master race consisted of gods while Jews were fit only for the gas chambers. The era of Fascism has led to the nations who suffered from it and survived it viewing with extreme suspicion all talk about innately superior or inferior human qualities. Yet extreme egalitarianism, or as I would prefer to term it, wrongly conceived egalitarianism, which ignores differences in capacities and achievement, has not served democracy well. Carried far enough, it means the lopping off of all heads which come above dead level. It means rule by committee because we distrust individual leadership, and it also means the end to that striving for excellence which has produced mankind's greatest achievements.

To summarize: in its moderate forms, the pursuit of equality prohibits ruthlessness in the strong, protects the weak from wanton injury and defines certain areas of equality which must not be transgressed. But it does not seek to eliminate individual differences or their consequences. This judicious insistence on equality has produced many measures which a modern democracy regards as vital – minimum wage laws, graduated income tax, the principle of one man one vote, the raising of the status of women.

62

But here is the dilemma. The very same society which stresses equality must, if it is not to sink from sight in a great swamp of mediocrity, encourage individual performance. I get great satisfaction from watching the children of poor homes, often denied an adequate education in colonial times, rise to the highest places in society through their own determined efforts. School textbooks contain many examples of great men and women in history who overcame grievous handicaps in order to enrich mankind by their talents and genius. But just as extreme egalitarianism has built-in dangers, so too has extreme emphasis on individual performance. It has produced such economic systems as capitalism with its total disregard for the weak and poor. That popular saying 'Everyone for himself and the Devil take the hindmost' is totally unacceptable in any State where absolute equality of opportunity is still far from realization. It gives the rich, the strong and the cunning a licence to become exploiters of the weak, the poor and the simple. No government, pledged to put Man at the centre of its policy-making and values, can tolerate the law of the jungle. Even within the law, power must be balanced against power – hence the economic power of the employer must be countered by the social power of the workers through trade unions. The consumer must be protected against profiteering and monopoly control of essential commodities. The ordinary citizen must have some champion against the exploitation of his lack of technical knowledge of the law, say, through a Law Society which regulates the ethics of those privileged to have extensive knowledge denied to the generality of citizens.

Of course, in a society of hereditary privilege such

as Northern Rhodesia in the old days or South Africa
at the present time, the underdog may not be happy
with his lot, but he develops acceptance because he has
no reason to look forward to any other fate. Never
having had the prospect of betterment, he reaches a
certain depth of disillusionment, shrugs his shoulders
and comes to terms with his situation. He entertains
neither hopes nor ambitions which cannot be realized
within the value system of such a society. But once the
oppressive regime is smashed, there is no ceiling on
expectations. Those with energy, ambition and talent
can meet any challenge. But there is the counter-danger
of unrealistic expectations which no government or
society could meet. So in the case of Zambia too many
people expected to inherit a house, a car and a salary
equal to that of the white man merely by virtue of the
lowering of the Union Jack and the raising of the
Zambian flag. Because this was plainly impossible there
was created a pressure of political frustration and
disillusionment with a Government which, however
well-intentioned, could not wave a magic wand and
transform society overnight, because it had to harmonize its policies with the harsh realities of economic
laws and social stability.

Thank God that the society in which you will grow
to maturity will have a much saner and more rational
understanding of the aspirations of its members and
infinitely more opportunities for the realization of these
aspirations. But I want to stress that this tension
between equality and individual performance can never
be fully resolved, and there is no shortage of unscrupu-
lous politicians who will prey on the despair of the
unfulfilled or the greed of the successful in order to

upset that delicate balance. Never having laboured
under the responsibilities of government leadership,
they can afford the luxury of proposing simplistic and
extreme solutions to social problems. Our economic
reforms over the past four years, which have been
vigorously attacked by those who had most to gain
under the old system of 'dog eat dog', have been aimed
at curbing the unwonted power of economic institutions
without going so far as to stifle that individual initiative
without which no industry, business or financial
organization can survive. It has been a hard struggle to
raise the floor beneath which no citizen could sink
without also lowering the ceiling so that those of
unusual stature were constricted and robbed of
effectiveness. The extent to which I have been successful
will be obvious as the years wear on. But do not make
the mistake, my dear children, of ignoring that built-in
tension between individual performance and equality
which I have dwelt upon at some length. The leader of
a nation such as ours is like a man driving two powerful and sometimes wild horses which want to dash off
in different directions but must be held together
somehow if they are to pull a load.

Excellence – that is the key-word of our endeavour,
and it must be honestly confessed that there are a good
many things in our character and national life which
are inimical to high standards – among them laziness,
complacency, greed, the reluctance to apply legitimate
discipline to the slack and incompetent. Those three
rights I mentioned earlier – to be, to have and to
belong, are easy enough to proclaim but a most intricate
system of checks and balances, governmental, political
and economic, are required to ensure their fulfilment.

The very transformations which technology has brought about in our society, not to mention other aspects of the social revolution through which we are living, have resulted in a nation whose operations are becoming so complex as to be baffling. And before us is the prospect of having to guide our country through changes even more radical than those we have so far seen. Only competence at every level within society can give us the outside hope of moving from the present to the future without collapsing into chaos or creating conditions of grave injustice.

The importance of excellence as a condition of freedom is too easily ignored, even by those of our citizens who should know better. An amiable fondness for the prizes of a free society is insufficient. Keeping a free society strong and vital is no job for the lazy or slovenly. Only men and women achieving excellence in whatever social or private station they find themselves can tone up our whole society. Those who are most deeply devoted to the ideals of a democratic society must be the ones who practice what they preach and show the highest standards of performance. Happy mediocrity will not do.

In essence, I am claiming that every citizen is, in the last resort, his own taskmaster. Free men set their own goals. Except where matters of central public policy are concerned, no one need tell citizens what to do; they must do it for themselves. They must be quick to apprehend the kinds of effort and performance their society needs, and they must demand that kind of effort and performance of themselves and their fellow citizens. They must cherish what has been called 'the habitual vision of greatness'. If they have the wisdom

66

and courage to demand much of themselves, they may look forward to living in, and passing on to their children, a society of strength and vitality. But a free society that is lax, passive and inert will not last long, and the mere fact of freedom will not save it.

I want to impress on you that freedom involves an arduous apprenticeship before it can be responsibly exercised. The unchanging requirement of any free society's survival is that each generation shall rediscover for itself this truth. The world will never be safe for democracy. It is always and everywhere in peril. It is eroded away most often not by the dramatic means of revolution so much as by the multitude of minor derelictions of duty by ordinary citizens who would be indignant if one accused them of treachery through laxity.

The survival of Zambian democracy depends on each of you setting for yourselves noble goals and then struggling to attain them. It is not the Party nor the Government nor the Legislature which is the final guardian of democracy, but the common man. And everything depends on our ability to get him to recognize the dignity of his role and the ultimate significance for the nation of his smallest actions.

Power – its use and abuse

I have written a lot about the power of this or the power of that, but now I want to give you my reflections on Power as such. There can be no more crucial issue in the modern world, and I want to teach you what experience has taught me about the use and abuse of this deadly commodity.

67

The time through which we are living could well be termed the Century of Power, for we have seen an intensification of man's age-old struggle for power. He has unlocked much of the power imprisoned in nature, and in the realm of human affairs he has created new and complex power structures. Internationally, the battle to maintain what is termed 'the balance of power' has reached crisis point: nations spend much of their substance in amassing the instruments of warlike power in the interests of what is called peace. National security and prestige demand the matching of power against power and still the deadly devices of nuclear destruction pour out even though there are already more than enough stockpiled to lay the world waste many times over.

Nationally, we have lived through a struggle for power in Africa which has centred round the drive for self-determination by indigenous peoples; a struggle which in Central Africa focused on the question – which race shall hold the reins of power and what protection will minorities have against the illegitimate use of power? Nationalism came to birth to challenge and finally overcome the force of imperialism, and now throughout the African continent north of the Zambezi, leaders are preoccupied with the complex problems associated with the use of the power which the people have placed in their hands.

Even at the personal level, the rise of popular psychology testifies to man's struggle to achieve self-mastery, to win the power to subdue his antisocial instincts and become a happy and mature personality. Whole schools of thought and new religions have offered cures for the fear which lack of personal power spells

68

out in neurosis, defeat and despair. Nostrums, therapies and ideologies compete to show man the key to unlock the power inherent in his personality.

We have seen power multiply in geometrical progression – a new manifestation here leading to an equal access of power there. Power to accomplish one's own purposes has given place to the power to match someone else's possession of it. I need power to protect myself against your misuse of power. The talk now is of countervailing power – the balancing of power against power to prevent exploitation. The economic power of the great corporation has demanded that the State must take to itself new powers in order to contain and keep it in check. In the realm of human affairs men have had to learn to control the explosion of new power which science and technology have offered. Indeed it would be true to say that power is no longer exercised in the open spaces of the world, as it were, to increase man's competence. Power has now expanded until it occupies all the available space and clashes with countervailing power: power unlocked from the world of nature is used to hold together the world community in a precarious balance of opposing forces.

Now, men may bewail the fact of the power struggle but there is no way in which they can avoid taking part in it. There is no possibility of disengagement. Was it not according to the Book of Genesis that Man was made the crown of Creation and given dominion over all created things? By virtue of this dominion Man has dignity, out of which he cannot contract, because he lives by God's power and indeed has to dispense some of it through his daily life. So Man by virtue of his divine creation, cannot take refuge in impotence.

69

Unlike the rest of the natural world, where the power relationships are clearly defined – each creature being both prey and predator – for Man, power is a spiritual problem. Each day he faces problems of decision making. To have dominion is an onerous thing: it calls for the handling of great power without being overcome by it.

Nor is Man's dominion confined to nature. There are hierarchies of power in human life; men exercise dominion over their fellow-men. Human society is a vast pyramid of power, of domination and subordination. This is the level at which the most crucial problems of power in the ethical field arise. Man is engaged in a power struggle from the cradle to the grave; it is inherent in the business of living. From the most intimate circle of his family to his membership of the widest ranging communities, Man has to make constant adjustments of power relationships, and those who pretend, for whatever reason, that they can turn their backs on this power struggle are living in a dream-world.

The inevitability of power is seen most clearly in political life. In the institution of the State, Man is confronted with power in the most absolute sense that can be known on earth. For the State must always have a monopoly of ultimate power – the power even of life and death over its citizens in order to maintain law and order. It is this monopoly of power alone which makes possible peace, order and justice. The State must always be in possession of 'power and to spare' so that it can, if necessary subdue all private pockets of power in the hands of individuals and institutions which would otherwise exercise arbitrary control over citizens. Law, which though guaranteed by the State, does not stem from it, is nothing other than 'ordered power'; that ordering comes ultimately from the sovereignty of God, in comparison with which all earthly sovereignty is conditional and limited.

It is because there is this recognition that all earthly sovereignty derives its legitimacy from God that in most States, the swearing-in ceremonies of high officials such as Heads of States, Justices and so on, involve some form of religious affirmation. The State is not the source of power; it merely mediates power derived from God.

There is no solution to the problems of power through States or individuals relinquishing it in order to make goodwill alone the basis of relationships. For when this happens men are at the mercy of the arbitrary power of private institutions. It is a myth that the citizen is more free in a weak State; indeed, where there is no framework of good order within which his freedom can be exercised, Man falls victim to anarchy and even chaos. And if there is one condition worse than totalitarianism, it is anarchy. At least in the totalitarian State, there is some kind of order, however harsh, but where anarchy rules every man preys on another like a wild beast.

Man is also confronted with the necessity for power in the sphere of politics. Every political problem is made up of both technical and moral elements, but the recitation of the clichés of simple moralism is no solution to political problems. All politics is power politics. Power is the ultimate sanction behind every political decision, for that decision is concerned with the means short of war by which relations between

individuals, groups and nations can be adjusted. Power
is the essential means by which things get done; the
material of political policies decide *what* things should
be done and in which order.

Power is, of course, ethically neutral. It all depends
who possesses it and to what purpose it is used. The
cobalt bomb in the hands of a medical specialist can be
used to cure cancer; its cousin, the hydrogen bomb, in
the hands of a power-drunk maniac could be used to
destroy the world. Yet it is the same power. Ethically
neutral though power may be, it exposes its possessor
to dangerous temptation – no one knows this better
than I do as the final repository of executive power at
the present time in the State of Zambia. The problem
of power is the other side of the question of freedom.
Power, having the capacity to compel, stands in direct
opposition to freedom. The surplus of freedom for one
man, which is power, is the deficit of freedom for
another man. Everything which has the capacity to
compel can become a means to power and so cause
men to lose their freedom by making them dependent on
the source of that power.

The attraction of power is that it extends the range
of a man's personality and allows him to fulfil himself
through the personalities of others. Power enables men
to multiply the impact of their personalities on the
world and other men. Hence it is often the source of
pride and arrogance. The absolute dictator uses the vast
power at his disposal to mould the lives of his subjects
to the point where they cease to be free persons and
become, as it were, limbs and organs of his own body;
his will expressed through theirs, his voice speaking
through their mouths.

72

Because power *works* where persuasion or goodwill
so often fail, it surrounds itself with an aura of prestige
which adds to its value. It becomes desirable not only
for what it is in itself and for what can be done with it,
but also for the awe and respect it calls out from weak
men. Power panders to a devilish pride because it makes
men both dependent and worshipful. Every man of
power finds himself surrounded by flatterers and
smooth talkers who respect him not for his own
personal qualities but because he has this magical thing,
however temporarily. Should he lose it or have it taken
from him, then, of course, the coterie of attendants
melts away and re-forms round whoever inherits the
reins of power.

Power is peculiarly desirable in the modern world
because it can be used to change the established order
of things in one's own favour. In former times, men
could use power legitimately to extend their influence
over unclaimed areas of life. Now, due to man's enterprise, the goods of this world have been fully apportioned
and so the will to power may find expression in theft –
the claiming of what is not one's own. This will
to power is seen most nakedly in territorial aggression,
but it operates just as effectively though more subtly
in the economic realm where it is dignified by terms
such as enterprise, expansion, development, when often
what is meant is greed, fraud or exploitation.

The most dangerous aspect of power is the insatiable
appetite it gives to many of those who possess it.
Edmund Burke once wrote: 'Those who have once
been intoxicated with power and have derived any
emolument from it, even though for a year, can never
willingly abandon it.' How true that is! Power is like

73

treacle; it sticks to one's fingers. It is greedy, constantly searching like the tongue of a lizard for fresh prey to devour. The world of power can so easily become a closed universe, cut off from the sources of morality, generating a fraudulent morality of its own, driving men in directions which, in their better moments, they would not take. I'm sure this is why Jesus warned that the rich will find it difficult to enter the Kingdom of God. Wealth is not evil in itself, but like every kind of power, it can destroy man's sense of dependence upon God. Money opens so many doors that the wealthy seem to think that the doors of Heaven will also yield before its pressures. Power apparently solves so many problems in this life that the powerful are tempted to believe that it solves them all, including that of our eternal destiny.

It must be obvious to you that I have learned by hard experience what a treacherous and yet necessary thing power is. Because the Zambian Constitution requires me to exercise great power, I engage in constant self-questioning and self-analysis to protect myself from the delusion that I am the one exception to the general rule that power corrupts those who use it. I vaguely remember reading about Plato's philosopher-kings who were apparently bred to the business of ruling their fellowmen. Only in absolute monarchies and English public-schools of the colonial era could such an arrogant assumption become the basis of statecraft. It is by an extraordinary train of events that I find myself in State House. I certainly do not believe that I was bred to rule over my fellow-Zambians – if anything I suspect I was bred to be a teacher or a farmer! So I do not expect God or Destiny to provide me with some

special dispensation to handle power with utter
innocence in the manner of those snake-charmers who
can tie cobras in knots without getting bitten.

So I have had to evolve what might somewhat
pompously be termed a philosophy of power – a set of
rough and ready rules by which to judge my own
performance and that of my fellow leaders. It is by no
means infallible, but better than nothing and so I want
to pass it on to you.

I try always to see that power is given a human face.
It is people who handle power and people who are on
the receiving end of it – therefore supreme power
must be vested in them. When this simple truth is
forgotten, those who are ruled make impossible
demands on their rulers who, in turn, become fas-
cinated with power for its own sake. My insistence that
Humanism must be taught in our schools and practised
in institutions such as trade unions and political parties,
industrial concerns and cooperatives is aimed at trying
to ensure that power is held in the control of wholesome character. For this is the nub of the problem of
power – the divorce between the fact of power and the
character of those exercising it.

Our century has seen an unprecedented increase in
power so that it seems that the very fire of the gods
rests in our hands. Yet much of the misery and
injustice of our time is the consequence of our failure
to develop the moral stature to be worthy of the degree
of power we control. So we live in constant fear of the
wild, destructive antics of technological giants who are
moral dwarfs. And if you think that is a pessimistic
estimate of mankind, then pick up a history book and
read the story of the twentieth century, which is a tale

of endlessly repeated human folly – before the last shot
of one war has been fired the stormclouds which herald
the next are already building up on the horizon. Even
in our own country, which by world standards is a
small one, I am constantly dismayed by the re-emer-
gence of the sins and attitudes which made colonialism
so oppressive. Did we rid ourselves of white oppressors
to put ourselves under the heel of black ones who have
developed identical appetites? Is it less tolerable for the
ordinary man to be at the mercy of a greedy black
capitalist than the white one whose place he has taken?
The misuse of power is a human problem; no race, class
or tribe has built-in immunity from its corrosive effects.

The key question of nation-building can be simply
posed. Is it possible to bring the springs of newly
acquired power under rational and benevolent control?
By the time the youngest of you is an adult and has
taken his place as a responsible citizen of Zambia, you
will know whether my generation mastered the power
at our disposal or became its slaves.

As I see it, only great characters are fitted to handle
great power. A cliché – but how true! Thrusting
through and beyond the technicalities of nation-building
is the imperative necessity to equip our people *morally*
to handle the varying degrees of power they are called
on to exercise. For this task we must marshall the
resources of the churches, our university, educational
system and every movement or organization that
touches the life of the people and can help mould their
character.

I know, probably better than anyone else in Zambia,
how formidable a task it is to give power a human face.
As the documents and files and reports pile higher and

higher on my desk, I have to fight my way through
them to get at the people who can so easily be buried
beneath these paper mountains. The problem of every
leader in a modern State is what might be termed that
of 'filtered experience'. He has to rely more and more
on what is reported to him, and because those who
produce the reports are human beings with their own
axes to grind, their own vested interests to protect, one
is too often told only what those who do the telling
imagine one wants to hear. I am not suggesting that
subordinates and aides are consciously dishonest. But
put at its lowest, they have jobs to protect, families to
feed, careers to advance, and these hard facts of life
inevitably colour their interpretation of policies and
events. A departmental minister, for example, is
unlikely to confront me with the words, 'I've made a
sorry mess of my job and you ought to fire me!' It is
even less likely that an official I myself have appointed
will pay me the compliment of utter candour and tell
me to my face that *I've* made a mess of something. Such
unpalatable truths are more likely to be hidden away in
a mass of statistics, a great collection of data – so that
both he and I have the excuse, should we wish to take
it, of blinding ourselves to an aspect of reality. And it
is the people, who are both the subject and object of all
policy, who pay the price for any rationalizing of failure.

I have worked out my own private system of
assessing the psychology of those whose task it is to
keep me informed of what is going on in the nation.
In fact, I have a threefold communications system.
There is the normal process of government and civil
service communication. Then, independently, there is
my network of direct links with Party officials, many

of them at the grass-roots, living and working among
the ordinary people. But equally important is my third
way of testing the mood of the nation and noting how
power is used at the point where it is applied to the
people – lightning and unheralded visits to a police
station, a hospital, a government office, to see for
myself how the common man is being treated. I regret
the panic such swift swoops may create in minor civil
servants or petty bureaucrats who suddenly find the
President's car arriving without warning outside their
office doors, but it is all part of the task of giving
power a human face. Within the limits of human
stamina and tight time schedules, I want to see for
myself how the policies my Party has initiated through
its Government are being carried out.

In the last resort, the leader of a nation is answerable
to the people, and he must spend as much time
amongst them as is practicable, given the multiplicity of
decision-making responsibilities which demand his
presence at the nerve centre of Government. There is
an unresolvable dilemma here. The people have the
right to greet and meet their President in their own
community, whether bustling city or rural village, *but*
the more time he spends *with* them the less time he has
available to work *for* them on matters of national
policy, which require leading and motivating the great
army of government officials in the capital. And I have
not even mentioned another function which a leader
neglects at his own and the nation's peril – winning
some time to *think*; just that, to think, to ponder, to
reflect, on a whole range of issues which may affect the
nation's future but have not at the time hardened into
policies and programmes.

I'm not really giving you a hard luck story about your father's tough life as President! There are compensations as well as challenges in the handling of power. But I do want you to have some insight into the pressures that have moulded my character, good or bad. Then at least you will be able to think charitably of me.

Another essential element in evolving a philosophy of power is to decide the relationship between power and purpose. Power is not an absolute thing. What is power-*ful* in one context may be power-*less* in another. In other words, those who must exercise power need constantly to engage in the process of clarifying their purposes – for that, in the end, is what power is – the ability to accomplish purpose. To use the wrong kind of power or an inappropriate degree of it may only frustrate one's best intentions and nullify one's goal. A sledgehammer will not rock a baby to sleep nor will a feather duster smash a steel barrier. In each case the form of power is out of harmony with the desired purpose.

Remembering always that I am thinking about power in relation to people, I believe that there are only two forms of power available for dealing with people. There is power *over* people – compulsion; and power *with* people – persuasion. Civilization itself can be seen from one angle as the attempt to replace power over people by power with people – compulsion by persuasion. I am always reluctant to use force of any kind so long as there is a possibility that persuasion may achieve the same end. My reading of history convinces me that truly great leaders are those who have been able to gain the respect of their followers to the extent

F

that an appeal is more powerful than a command. To drive men where they would not willingly follow is always a last resort because, with the exception of those of evil intent, it is a violation of their personalities, and must also be seen as a failure of leadership. I dare to hope that one fruit of my leadership of this nation will be the emergence of a people easy to lead but difficult to drive; easy to govern but impossible to enslave.

So whether our new nation has the power it needs depends on the purposes it intends to serve. And this brings us back again to those broad, fundamental questions about where our nation is going; what we intend Zambia to *be*. Only by constant discussion, debate and education can we clarify our ultimate purposes. This is the process which is prior to all policy making and the drawing up of Party programmes.

I'm haunted always by the fear that the massive power the nation has entrusted to me may be wasted in futile acts of self-glorification or violate the integrity of those who are on the receiving end of such power. For me, Humanism is not only an attempt to clarify the fundamental purposes to which power should be dedicated but also a check on that aggressive instinct which I share with all men. Sometimes I succeed, sometimes I fail, but always I try to wear down the ill-will of my opponents by patient persuasion before bringing to bear the naked power of the Presidential Office to compel obedience to the law and spirit of our Constitution.

This brings me to perhaps the most difficult lesson I have had to learn about the handling of power – the relationship between power and patience. And this is something you yourselves taught me in the intimacy of our family circle. Every wise parent learns that though he has the physical strength to compel his children to obey him, if he hopes to get a childlike personality to mature, he must refrain from using such power in the belief that patient example is a better teacher than the whip. The parent–child relationship is one common example of the truth that the test of mastery of power is the willingness to refrain from using it. It may sound paradoxical, but experience has taught me that such a gamble can pay off. And what I learned in our family circle I have often used with profit in the larger area of national and international policy. Indeed, is it not one sign of the growing maturity of the community of nations that diplomacy has replaced physical aggression as a means of regulating relations between peoples? The willingness to talk and talk and keep on talking when it might be both simpler and also apparently more impressive to use military might to resolve deadlocks is a great sign of hope in world affairs.

Someone has said that war is diplomacy carried on by other means. May be so; but war is always a tragically inferior form of diplomacy. The test of a nation's control of power is the ease or otherwise with which it can be needled into using it. Like the Apostle Paul's description of love, true power is 'not easily provoked'. And thank God for national leaders who have shown great forbearance in the face of provocation and so spared the world from awful blood-letting.

To exercise great patience in the use of power demands that one should be an optimist about the nature of one's fellow men. Because I believe that there is rationality and nobility in Man's character, I am prepared to take the risk of appealing to his better self before embarking upon a policy of regimentation. Obviously, if a leader dismisses his people with contempt as little more than slaves or a superior species of brute creation, then he will throw his weight around and attempt to achieve his goals by the indiscriminate use of force. Though I have had my disappointments and setbacks, in general my regard for my fellowmen has increased over time, and so I have never felt the compulsion to exercise power like a despot. And I do everything possible to persuade my colleagues that the precipitate use of power can only lead to their forfeiting the people's respect with the result that a liberal democracy degenerates into a totalitarian regime. For those whom the people do not respect they will obey only with the greatest reluctance. Furthermore, no State which is founded and maintained by the arbitrary use of force can survive indefinitely. Sooner or later, the people will react against the brutalization of their true natures and smash the system that has tyrannized them. Violent revolutions have one thing in common – it is the people meeting blow for blow and taking back by force the power they entrusted to their leaders and which has been used to restrict their freedom and deny them self-fulfilment.

I should not be in the least bit surprised if, in later life, you heard it claimed that Kaunda was weak; that he should have used force to destroy his political opponents or meet the provocation of hostile nations. Even on the domestic front, I get no shortage of advice from all quarters that there are certain policies I ought to push through for the people's good, regardless of the people's will. So be it. Let history

judge both my motives and my performance. For my
own part, I would like to believe that it is patience rather
than weakness which has caused me to exercise only
with the greatest reluctance the tremendous power
which the Constitution places in the keeping of the
President. Only when I regretfully conclude that an
appeal to a man's better nature has failed will I invoke
the full rigour of the powers of my Office. It is a
narrow line which divides patience from weakness and
those who choose to walk that line will suffer calumny
and scorn, but their duty is plain: to use power if they
must but persuasion if they can.

No doubt my critics will take great delight in
pointing out that on a number of occasions I have used
my special power as President to detain or restrict
political opponents without trial. These critics neither
know nor care what such measures have cost me in
grief and anguish. Some of Zambia's political prisoners
have been colleagues who fought beside me in the
freedom struggle and in some cases have shared the
joys and sufferings of my early life. Well, no excuses
and no self-justification! There are times when even the
most liberal and democratic of States must restrict the
freedom of its citizens in what seems to be an arbitrary
fashion. If the very existence of the nation is threatened;
if there is real danger of national unity fragmenting
into tribal and regional anarchy; if outside enemies
threaten the State's survival and use dissident elements
within it as their tools, then in the name and for the
sake of all citizens the Government may have to take
strenuous action against some citizens. In Western
liberal democracies it is universally conceded that in
time of war or national emergency the survival of the

State must take priority over other values such as freedom of expression and the right of unlimited opposition. Many of the nations of Southern Africa are in a constant state of undeclared war. So at times the President must act with a degree of rigour he may bitterly regret but which he cannot avoid without forfeiting the responsibilities of his office and abandoning his people to anarchy or widespread subversion.

It is part of the pain of power that those who exercise it must not allow the ties of past friendship to deter them from actions which may cause private anguish and inflict secret scars. Where the welfare of the people is involved, a leader is not allowed the luxury of friends entitled to special treatment or particular exemption from the obligations of loyalty to the State. And be it said, what applies to friends applies equally to one's own family. For me, Zambia comes first: all other loyalties and affections take second place. That is a terrible confession for any father and husband to make, but I make it in deadly seriousness, daring to hope that you will understand and forgive.

Let me, by way of a postscript on this discussion of power, add a word or two about power in the most personal sense. Most great religions teach that there is a huge storehouse of untapped power locked away in every man. Only a tiny fraction of this power is used constructively; the rest either remains dormant or is unleashed for destructive purposes. Aren't we all capable of expending demonic energy in hatred, selfishness and jealousy? This is power gone to waste, working itself out to the hurt of one's self and one's fellows. The truly mature personality not only keeps its inherent power under strong moral control but also uses it to the full for socially desirable purposes.

There is the power of the intellect, which is not merely intelligence but also the force of a strong mind which can cut through the complexities of issues and expose their inner core of meaning. There is also great spiritual power in the human personality which can release a person from self-preoccupation; set him beyond the reach of the base and low and make him king over his own being. There is also the power of will. This is the gift of steadfastness. How sorely our nation lacks this quality! How easily we get discouraged, abandon our long-term goals and settle for short-term successes. How often I have told our people in my public speeches that there is no room for shortlived enthusiasms in the work of nation-building! It is one thing to *want* something worthwhile; quite another to *will* it. A great nation is not the creation of a day and a night but of generations – each generation passing on to the one which succeeds it a vision and enthusiasm which unfavourable circumstances may from time to time damp down but cannot totally extinguish.

It is my prayer for you that you will unlock the power inherent in your personalities and use it both to become individually fulfilled and also make a mark on our nation. Do not fear power, but never cease to respect it, aware both of the dangers and opportunities it offers those who are prepared to risk using it.

Freedom and its limits

The discussion of power leads me naturally on to say something about freedom. The continent into which

85

you were born is obsessed with the idea of freedom. In one colonial territory after another, the urge to be free has nerved thousands to suffer and indeed to die. The rallying cries of freedom have awakened sleeping peoples to a sense of new destiny and set them marching along the road to self-determination. The saga of Black Africa's freedom struggle will be a matter of history by the time you are adult, but the desire to enlarge the areas of human freedom will remain for generations to come a dominant theme in human aspirations. *Freedom* is undoubtedly the hardest-worked word in the entire vocabulary of politics. Yet so many different things are meant by it, that the word might well qualify for inclusion in the grammar book of Humpty Dumpty in *Alice Through the Looking Glass*, who said that a word meant precisely what he wanted it to mean, neither more nor less.

If only freedom were as simple as many people, especially politicians, make out! To listen to their speeches, you would imagine that freedom is as natural as sunshine or air – a constituent of life which every man has unless he is forcibly deprived of it. This is a delusion, just as it is a delusion to believe that freedom means doing what you like without restraint, pursuing one's own ambitions without regard to others, coveting their property, their wealth or their jobs! We won't easily forget those Black politicians who tried to sweep to power after Independence on the specious promise that they would share out to every black Zambian the houses, jobs and bank balances of the expatriates they would drive away from the country. Fortunately, most of our people had better sense than to be taken in by such nonsense. But it was no easy task to educate the

86

masses into a realization that freedom is no magical
state of earthly bliss accomplished by a stroke of the
pen in the act of signing an Independence instrument.

A complex balance of conditions is necessary to
make freedom a reality, and a number of misconcep-
tions have to be cleared out of the way before it is
possible to get the people to realize what a hard,
burdensome thing is this freedom they demand as a
right. Take, for instance, the idea of freedom as
self-will. The *Oxford Dictionary* defines freedom as the
condition of 'not being subject as a slave to a master' –
which suggests that freedom is the ability to do what
one likes, driven on by one's desires and ambitions.

For thousands this is what freedom means – the right
of self-disposal; to dream one's own dreams, follow
one's own star and snap one's fingers at any attempt to
impose a superior will. And very nice too – unless one
realizes that such a view of freedom has three consequences that are personally and politically destructive.
First, it leads to self-idolatry. Only God is, by
definition, self-entire, self-directed and totally without
claims against himself. The assumption that freedom
means complete independence of any outside force,
sanction or personality is both a blasphemy and a
delusion. Secondly it is a denial of the social good for
where the individual's will is sovereign, there is no
possibility of harmonizing all the wills within society
through a process of compromise and sacrifice. The
freedom of each becomes destructive of the freedom of
others, and there occurs a series of clashes like the
fighting of animals for the right to a waterhole or a
prize piece of a carcass. Thirdly, self-will as a philosophy tends inevitably towards totalitarianism. Men

who are not prepared to give up some of their
freedom end up losing all of it.

Though this is not a popular idea, Man is intended
to be both master and servant. Even if he manages to
throw off all external restraints, he still becomes prey
to his bodily functions and material needs. He is at the
mercy of his instincts and those powerful drives which
originate deep within his personality. Indeed, if the
self-willed man is mastered by nothing else, he will be
mastered by the idea of self-will – freedom itself will
become a tyrant. Freedom then is not the absence of
any outside control; it is the acceptance of spiritual as
opposed to mechanical or organic limitations. By the
very fact of existing at all, Man is spiritually conditioned. His path can never be as free as that of an
airborne bird. He must pick his way painfully through
a veritable jungle of alternatives, few of which are
satisfactory, none of which is perfect. Man can never
be the unconditional master of himself because he
neither has complete control of himself nor of his
environment. He is at the mercy of dreams, hopes,
fears and lusts. So that self-will which poses as freedom
will only result in a man putting himself under the heel
of some subtle tyranny more frightening than any of
those from which he fondly imagines he has freed
himself.

The second faulty conception of freedom is the idea
of absence of external restraints. In modern usage, the
word 'freedom' is usually followed by the preposition
'from' – freedom *from* fear, freedom *from* ignorance,
freedom *from* war, and so on. In fact, the word freedom
ought always to be associated with the preposition
'for' – freedom *for* various forms of service. In other

words, freedom is not something a man possesses in the same way that he possesses friends or property or talents. It is not an end in itself. Freedom is a by-product of service and must be blended with obedience to produce responsibility. The truly free man is not at liberty to do as he likes. His values, his scruples and fundamental goals place limitations on what he can do with himself and his gifts. This noble conception of freedom is not easily attained. It demands sacrifice and virtue and a perpetual victory of man over himself. We are free not *from* various evils, but free *for* various forms of service.

We sometimes use the word 'freedom' and 'liberty' as though they meant the same and were interchangeable. Of course they are not. In the ultimate sense a man might still be truly free even though deprived of his liberty. His spirit might not be in chains even though his body is. Think, for example, of the great literature which has been written by men in gaol – Bunyan's *Pilgrim's Progress*, Paul's *Epistles* – to give just two examples. These works issued from the unconquered spirits of free men. Their bodily confinement was an unpleasant incidental. By the same token a man can be at liberty and yet not be truly free – he may be enslaved to his emotions, his bodily desires, or even to evil ideas that have captured his mind even though he is nominally liberated. Men may have liberty in ignorance, not knowing how or why they possess it, merely enjoying it. Freedom implies knowledge. Men must know *why* they are free in order to enlist themselves to some cause that makes their freedom worth while.

Personal liberty is the idol of the modern world. It is the one value in defence of which men still feel

justified in going to war. Yet every modern State,
whether democratic or totalitarian, finds it necessary
from time to time to place restrictions on personal
liberty. Some observers, for example, view with
foreboding the emergence of the one-party democracy,
the restriction of the operation of opposition parties,
the ruthless harnessing of national resources to meet
primary challenges. It may be unpalatable for some
purists to be told that there are times in those perilous
first days of independence when total liberty is a
luxury the new nation cannot afford. At this point, the
distinction between freedom and liberty becomes
vitally important. We must somehow come to understand how it is possible for men to be truly free when
serving a dedicated nation that puts restraints on
their liberty. Desperate necessity decrees that the State
must survive; that it must resist the pressures towards
tribal division or the threat of external subversion.
Even an authoritarian State can provide a theatre for
personal service. I cannot believe that a lazy Westerner,
luxuriating in the possession of personal liberties he
hardly ever exercises, is any more free than the citizen
of a new nation conscripted to meet the challenge of
desperate necessity in his own land.

What, in sum, I am saying is that obedience is the
highest exercise of freedom. The crown of the evolutionary process is not Man but Responsible Man, and
responsibility is the tension between freedom and
obedience. Responsibility is the constructive use of
freedom. Man is given freedom in order to obey. The
rogue man who offers obedience to no one may be at
liberty, but he can never be truly free. The essence of
obedience is neither fear of punishment nor hope of

reward, but consent. Where obedience is by consent, there is no loss of freedom when men voluntarily accept the restriction of their liberties. Freedom and obedience are two sides of the same coin. Freedom without obedience is self-will, while obedience without freedom is slavery. Africa greatly needs this word about the possibility of uniting freedom and obedience because the hard facts of life will only yield before the efforts of men who are prepared to make a willing response to the challenge of desperate necessity; who will make what has to be done the thing they want to do.[1] The vast and intimidating problems which are tearing our continent apart can only be solved by the association of human ability, lavishly given, with the will to survival.

Freedom is also necessarily related to truth in the most elementary sense. Man needs freedom in order to be rational; to take part in the life of the mind. He needs freedom to win knowledge from the world, to plan, predict and analyse; to extend the frontiers of knowledge. Freedom is necessary to the life of the mind because truth is advanced by competition amongst ideas. As in the world of the beasts, so in the mental world there is a sort of survival of the fittest in operation; the toughest, most flexible ideas finally triumph when schools of thought clash. Indeed, truth is the infallible test of real freedom. The question we must ask is: does what we fondly imagine to be freedom take us nearer to the truth; does it increase the possibility of our believing, hoping and loving?

So a true understanding of the nature of freedom is not some flimsy thing of light and air. Freedom is

[1] I have developed these ideas more fully in my *Humanist in Africa*, Longmans, 1966.

really a burden laid on men. It constitutes their greatest hardship as well as their greatest glory. Those who ask for freedom must be aware what it is they are demanding. The prisoner or slave may not be at liberty but he has security, a roof over his head at night, a little food. Freedom on the other hand is first of all the freedom to suffer and if necessary to die. There's a modern version of an old Negro spiritual which is sung by young blacks in the US Freedom Movement. It goes like this:

I woke up this morning with my mind on freedom
Alleluyah
Ain't no harm to keep your mind on freedom
Alleluyah
I'm gonna walk, talk with my mind on freedom
Alleluyah
I'm singing and praying with my mind on freedom
Alleluyah

It thrills me to hear those young people singing bravely that old slave melody – the urge to be free is now a world-wide movement and nothing can, in the long run, stop it. But just possibly because my hair's turned white in the struggle for freedom, I might with great humility say to those young people and all like them: Be sure you know what you are asking for when you demand freedom. Through all your exhilaration and idealism always keep one sobering thought in the deep recesses of your mind – freedom is a burden laid upon the backs of those strong enough to carry it. The price of freedom is obedience, discipline, self-denial. And the most important question of all is: what are you going to do with it when you've got it?

Justice and law

And the almost universal answer that young people
will return to that question I have just posed: what
will you do with your freedom when you get it? will
have to do with justice and equality. And so it should.
To me, justice is a precious thing because most of my
life has been taken up with the struggle for it. Even
as a schoolboy I was a thorn in the flesh of the missionaries who taught me at school and of the District
Commissioners who ruled the area where we lived. I
was often given a thrashing for daring to challenge
the authority of the white man. I did not then, and I
do not now doubt his good intentions, but I often felt
that his wisdom was flawed by unconscious racial bias.
I was fighting for justice long before I could have
defined the word. I just *knew* that I and my kind were
not getting a fair deal. And this taught me a lesson I
have often applied since in the business of statecraft
– that it is often those who are denied justice who have
the clearest idea where justice lies. Often, though not
always, people who are burning with resentment
because they are denied certain things to which they
feel entitled are a surer guide to the nature of true
justice than the appropriate chapter in some textbook
of political theory.

One of the earliest definitions of justice I ever read
was from the works of Aristotle. Justice, he claimed,
means giving to every man his due. It didn't take me
very long to discover the snag in that formula. It took
no account of the selfishness which plays some role in

every human action. In other words, I may be alert to circumstances in which I receive less than my due, but not equally sensitive to the fact that *you* are being treated unjustly. And indeed, there may be situations in which it is just not possible for both myself and yourself to receive our due. Anyway, who decides what is my due?

The business of statecraft has undoubtedly been made more rational and probably easier by the evolution of a general consensus as to what are the basic rights any State ought to guarantee its citizens. To those basic *human* rights set out in the post-revolutionary constitutions of France and the United States and in the Charter of the United Nations, there have been added a list of *political* rights which it would be generally conceded a State ought to offer to its citizens if it is to qualify as humane and democratic – the right to active participation in political life, to a measure of consent in the form of government, to free association and free debate: all this, backed by an independent judiciary. I think we are also feeling our way towards some statement of the *economic* rights of a free man as it has become clear that the operation of economic forces can be productive of gross injustice.

Since those schoolboy days I have had to do a lot of thinking about justice. I have, for example, the dubious distinction of having been a jail-bird so I know something about crime and punishment from first-hand experience! But now I find myself at the heart of a whole complex network of institutions and relationships that have to do with justice. I must be both law-maker and law-dispenser, the one who appoints judges and also the final court of appeal from their decisions. It is an awesome responsibility which I often wish I need not exercise. But experience has taught me that it is never enough to struggle against specific evils; one must also try to create an environment which is hospitable to the growth of the corresponding virtues. All societies are dynamic, constantly in a state of flux, so that the passing of time can transform today's virtue into tomorrow's vice. Hence, the battle for justice is never won once and for all; the same battle has to be fought over and over again. The ground may be different, the weapons more sophisticated, but the war is never ending.

What, then, are the characteristics of justice? By what yardstick do I decide that our laws and my own decisions are not arbitrary and prejudiced? Obviously the *content* of a just decision or law will be as variable as the variety of situations to which it must respond; but the *context* of justice ought to be constant.

In the first place justice must be *impersonal* in the sense that it ignores the wealth, class, tribe or wisdom of those who seek it. This can often be a difficult principle to incorporate in modern legal systems in Africa if only because there is a longstanding tradition in many tribes that showing partiality towards one's relatives is in no way to be condemned as favouritism. It is one of those privileges which is the other side of the coin to the network of obligations into which one enters as a member of the extended family. Obviously, even in the most impersonal system of justice there will be occasions when account must be taken not only of human actions but also of personal circumstances. In such cases, my own view is that the trend of justice should always be towards leniency rather than severity, for the obvious reason that neither judges nor legal system can ever claim infallibility. There is always the possibility of the judicial system being the instrument of injustice, however unintentional. This being so, I personally would rather live with the frustration of suspecting someone had got less than his just deserts than with the anguish of fearing that anyone had become the victim rather than the beneficiary of our judicial system.

Secondly, it seems to me that *constancy* is an essential element in justice. The greatest weakness of any legal system is inconsistency and the worst vice in any judge is capriciousness. The State must not appear to condemn today what it approved yesterday. Any exceptions to general rules must *be* exceptional, otherwise that strong network of mutual obligations which binds all citizens disintegrates and the shadow of anarchy is abroad in the land. Justice has been described as 'the hard, general and rational skeleton of a community indwelt by sin'. The characteristic of a skeleton is to provide a framework which alone ensures that the organism does not collapse. The State is a community defined, strengthened and tempered by justice.

Certainly, when I define justice in terms of constancy I am not suggesting that law is immobile, once and for all. If this were so, then at the very least it would suggest both that the Government was doing no creative political thinking and also that the conscience of the community had atrophied. But change in the law must be *rational* so that citizens who take the trouble to find out can see why such changes have taken place. In particular, it is important that those with a certain degree of intelligence and criticial knowledge can understand how and why judicial decisions are made.

96

Societies where the law-givers are an elite, whether
aristocratic or religious, who make decisions in a
totally arbitrary fashion, are always backward because
their members are denied a fundamental human
privilege – that of doing right by intention – and are
also robbed of the assurance that they are not at the
mercy of irrational power.

But in order to be rational, justice must also be *open*.
The State has such vast power at its disposal that its
actions should, as far as is consistent with national
security, be exposed to the light of day. Whoever in
authority is beyond the scrutiny of the citizens is
exposed to every temptation of the corruptions of
power. This applies particularly to those who dispense
justice. Secret courts may, on occasion, be a regrettable
necessity, but when they become a general rule, the
State is in mortal danger. That dictum which has
become a cliché about justice not only being done but
also being seen to be done applies with special force to
the new nations where the tradition of representative
democracy may be novel and ill-understood by the
common people. The only way to prevent a return to
the rule of either the tribal *cabal* or the colonial minority
is for the people to be able to observe the mechanics of
government in operation and recognize that what they
see is demonstrably for the public good. It was Aristotle
a long time ago who wrote that Nature does nothing
in vain and so gave men the power of speech rather
than the meaningless grunts of the animals so that they
could converse about what is just and unjust and so
develop common sentiments and loyalties to cement
the unity of the State.

I have given you this long lecture on political theory, because I am anxious that you should be well informed and sensitive citizens of our society. Most of the things I have learned about these great values have come not from textbooks but out of my varied experience as politician, administrator and citizen. Whether my ideas are superficial or profound I have no way of knowing because frankly I am much too busy trying to do my job as Head of State to spare time to do a degree in political science. All I know is that they *work*; that acknowledging the fact I have made mistakes and fallen short of my high vocation, these ideas I have been trying to articulate have been and remain the raw material of my political philosophy. Some of you, given the benefit of a better formal education than I received, may find them crude. So be it. All I would beg you to remember is that there is all the difference in the world between being an expert in the theory of Government and having to run one. At the very least, this exposition of my ideas on freedom, power and justice will have a certain historical interest for those who come after me. These things I have believed, and for better or for worse, have tried to put them into practice during the perilous early years of Zambia's existence.

Long-term goals: world community

I want to share with you some of my thoughts about the long-term goals of mankind. You will grow up to be not only citizens of Zambia and children of Africa but also people of a world struggling to find wholeness

98

and unity. I must confess that when I was younger I felt that world-government might become a reality in my own life-time. The political unification of the world seemed so *obvious* a cure for the persistent ills of mankind – recurrent wars, damaging economic competitiveness and gross disparities in the distribution of the earth's resources. I made that most understandable of all mistakes of the young (from which the old, too, are not immune!), of assuming that because something is desirable it must also, by definition, be possible.

Now I know better. My ideal remains untarnished; it is my realistic expectations that have been cut down to size by observing and sharing in the moulding of one nation from a collection of tribes and races contained within arbitrarily drawn colonial boundaries. My experience too, of Pan-African diplomacy, has made me realize just how difficult it is to overcome long-standing hostilities, harmonize alien cultures and religions and subordinate national pride to some larger loyalty. And let me at this point pay tribute to the memory of Kwame Nkrumah who died recently in exile. In the longer perspectives of history, I am confident that he will overshadow the controversies which presently attach to his name and period of rule over Ghana. He deserves the title of first Citizen of Africa because he never abandoned his vision of a United States of Africa in which the resources of the entire continent would be available to cope with its problems. In this, I believe he was entirely right, and I pledge myself, as have many of my fellow-leaders, to the same goal.

But it would be foolhardy to underestimate the obstacles which block that narrow path which some day will broaden into a great highway. And what is true of Africa must apply with even greater force to the ideal of world community. Westerners are always talking about the Third World, the wretched habitation of the have-nots. In fact, there are many worlds, a bewildering variety of national and regional groupings which reflect the fragmented human condition at any given time. How do we fight our way forward from many worlds to one world? That is the question which haunts twentieth-century Man and I am afraid it will probably preoccupy Man in the twenty-first century as well. And in personal terms, some of you, my children, will be citizens of that twenty-first century.

My thoughts, for what they are worth, are these.

Technology has established a rudimentary world community but we have not yet devised the means of creating moral and political integration. This being so, economic interdependence in the absence of mutual trust and respect has served to sharpen already existing divisions. Because there is not yet, in spite of the valiant efforts of the United Nations Organisation (of which I am an enthusiastic supporter), a corpus of international law backed by effective sanctions, the poor and weak nations are naked and defenceless before the greed and self-interest of powerful and wealthy countries whose affluence is largely achieved at our expense. That is a lamentable fact of life at the present time.

And yet my numerous journeyings throughout both Western and Eastern power blocs give me some cause for hope. I sense a growing revulsion among the young against the policies of self-aggrandizement pursued by their elders who determine the destiny of

the rich nations. It is, of course, sneeringly affirmed
that the young, once middle-age overtakes them,
imperceptibly develop Establishment attitudes and
appetites. Possibly; though I detect in the air of our
time a volume of social energy and untapped idealism
which in the correct proportions might become
explosive and shatter once and for all this hitherto
inevitable progression from young dynamism to elderly
conservatism.

But for all the undeniable evidences of a sharpened
conscience amongst the young, the truth is that we
have not yet created the social tissue out of which a
supranational State can evolve. Even the confident
Marxist predictions of the 1920s that communist
ideology would unite the world has resulted in a proli-
feration of States as diverse as Guinea, Yugoslavia,
Russia and China, all of which seem to exhibit symptoms
of distinctive nationalism, even though each incor-
porates a Red Star in its national emblem.

There are those who claim that the threat of mutual
annihilation has the paradoxical effect of forcing an
uneasy kind of world community into existence. It
would be foolish to underestimate the extent to which
the fact of nuclear weapons has brought a new element
of responsibility into the conduct of international
affairs. But it must be sadly recorded that history has
no record of different peoples establishing common
community because they feared each other. Indeed,
recent events on the Indian subcontinent have been a
bitter setback to the exponents of world community
because we have seen the inhabitants of one land mass
splinter into hostile States.

Still, in spite of the wars and rumours of wars that

devastate the earth and scar the soul of Man; despite
the dismal evidence furnished by the failure of the UN,
the OAU, the Commonwealth, or any other international
organization, to reconcile the hostilities of their members (though I think the successes of such peace-making
agents taken in sum are more impressive than the
apostles of pessimism will allow) I still passionately
believe that the ideal of world community has taken
hold of the human imagination. And there are firmer
evidences still. Science especially is a great internationalizing force. Its conclusions are known to all, its
methods are open to all and its results increasingly
available to all. And men of science become more and
more impatient with the politicians or industrialists
who want to restrict the fruits of their work for
reasons of security or profit. It is, I think, no accident
that a considerable number of so-called traitors in the
postwar world have been scientists, determined at whatever cost to make contact and exchange information with
colleagues in nations politically hostile to their own.

Similarly, music and art fulfil an important role in
helping to break down the prejudice, arrogance and
exclusiveness of the old nationalist sentiment. True,
this is an agonizingly slow process, but I do see the
shadowy outlines of world community emerging from
such human activities. There is the internationalizing of
knowledge; the evolution of a common conscience so
that the moral enormities that occur do bring down on
the nations which perpetrate them the condemnation of
the world community. There are increasing areas of
joint action, particularly in helping the victims of great
disasters – earthquake, famine, tornado. But all this is a
long way short of any sort of world government.

Being a humanist I believe that the search for true
international community has to be pursued on two
fundamental levels. On the one hand we must do all
we can to strengthen the authority of organizations
like the United Nations, and extend our own links with
other nations in such areas as economic development,
foreign policy and defence. But at the most personal
level we must do everything possible by way of
education and example to translate the reality of
mankind from the imagination of Man to his soul, or
rather, his psychology, so that he begins to think more
in terms of the things which unite him to other men
than the things which divide him from them.

I am hesitant to use the term, but I do believe in the
need to propagate a religion of humanity which in no
way negates the morally elevating aspects of the great
world religions but correlates their deepest insights into
Man's nature. I envisage the service of God as being
most practically effected through the service of one's
fellow men. No earthly idol, whether the State, the
family or anything else, ought to take priority over
respect for mankind; they are only worthy of respect
in so far as they are images of the human spirit,
enshrine its presence and aid its self-fulfilment. But
where the cult of these idols seeks to usurp the place of
the spirit, they should be put aside. Indeed, they *will* be
put aside. They become dead husks, destined to decay.
No injunctions of old creeds, religious, political, social
or cultural, are valid if they diminish Man. Science
even, one of the chief idols of the modern world, must
not be allowed to serve any lesser goal than the greater
humanizing of Man. War, the needless taking of human
life, cruelty of all kinds, whether committed by the

State or the individual, the degradation of any human being, class or race, under whatever specious plea or justification, are intolerable crimes against the religion of mankind, abominable to its ethical mind, forbidden by its primary tenets, to be fought against always and tolerated not at all. Man must be sacred to man. The body of man is to be respected, made immune from violence and outrage, protected by science against disease and preventable death. The life of man is to be held sacred, preserved, ennobled and uplifted. The heart of man is to be held sacred also, given scope for love, protected against dehumanizing influences that would turn it into some biological machine. The mind of man is to be released from all bonds, given freedom and opportunity to use the full range of its powers in the service of mankind.

All this I believe with an intensity that moves me to terrible anger when I see Man misused, degraded and abandoned to the mercy of impersonal forces. These apparently abstract sentiments have, in fact, been the driving power behind much that mankind has accomplished through men and women of many races and all ages. In so far as society has been humanized, its concepts of work, of law and punishment, of the treatment of the weak and underprivileged enlightened, it is exponents of this religion of mankind who have accomplished these things. They have stimulated philanthropy and charity, put a curb on oppression and minimized its most brutal aspects.

It is from this source deep in the soul of the individual that I believe the creative power to achieve world community must come. And the great enemy of the religion of mankind is egotism, whether of the

individual, the race or the nation. Until enough men
recognize that the fulfilment of the human spirit is
impossible in isolation from the fulfilment of all men,
then the most pessimistic predictions about the future
of the human race will prove accurate and for all the
dazzling light of science we shall enter a new Dark Age.

So what I am trying desperately hard to impress
on you while you still burn with the idealism and
enthusiasm of youth is that no mechanical, political
or administrative unity of mankind is remotely possible
until the sacred value of Man possesses not only your
imaginations as a vision but also your wills as a
programme of action and a way of life.

The old evangelists like my revered father, who
never lived to witness the marvels of this modern age,
were, for all their blessed simplicity, utterly justified
in their claim that all social, political and economic
programmes for the betterment of the human condition
finally depend on a fundamental change in human
nature. As a boy, I remember him thundering from that
pulpit in Lubwa, that all men must be brothers, but
how is that possible unless they acknowledge a common
Father? True brotherhood, which is the final, far-off
goal of the human race, is ultimately dependent
upon what my Indian friends would call soul force.
Brotherhood exists only in the soul and by the soul.
It can exist by nothing else. For all men are *not* brothers
by biological kinship, human association or intellectual
agreement. They are brothers at the level of the soul;
and all forms of human unity, political, social and
economic, can only be expressions of soul brotherhood;
never substitutes for it.

My theologian friends tell me it is unfashionable

these days to talk about the soul. So much the worse
for theology! For I believe that the soul is the seat of
all social virtue. When the soul claims freedom, it is the
freedom of its self-development, the self-development
of the divine in Man in all his being. When it claims
equality, what is being claimed is that same freedom
equally for all and the recognition of the same soul,
the same divinity in all human beings. When it strives
for brotherhood, it is founding that equal freedom of
self-development on a common aim, a common life, a
unity of mind and feeling.

So when I talk of the human soul, I am using that
term to describe the primal essence of a man as the
centre of a network of relationships with others. This
is why I contrast ego with soul and regard egotism
as the great enemy of mankind. When the ego claims
liberty, it arrives only at competitive individualism.
When it asserts equality, it succeeds only in creating a
mechanical uniformity of society which suppresses
the infinite variations of human types from whose
interaction creativity, beauty and excitement flourish.
Hence a society of egotists which pursues liberty is
unable to achieve equality; the same society which aims
at equality is obliged to sacrifice liberty. For the
egotistic personality to speak of fraternity is to talk
of things contrary to its nature. The egotism of men
can be neutralized, balanced and harmonized in such
a way that some kind of community is possible.
Obviously this is so, otherwise I would not be writing
this and you would not be reading it! But I am sure
that the apparently inviolate law of growth and decay
which characterizes societies at present can only be
broken and some form of lasting and all-embracing

community created when sufficient people realize that
the revolution which really has lasting effect is not
that which is achieved from the outside in – that is
by violent economic and political change altering
human nature – but from the inside out – human nature
being transformed so that men create societies worthy
of their stature as Man made in the image of God.

And I end this rather odd discussion about the
possibility of world community by putting to you
my conviction that the challenge which will face
your generation when it rules the world can be stated
in a question simple to express though desperately
difficult to answer. How can we get men to live from
their soul instead of their ego? I would suggest, with
the diffidence of one who will have had his day and
ceased to be, that in this struggle the role of religion
will be crucial. It would not be putting it too highly
to claim that if, as is commonly assumed, religion is
finished, then Man is finished, and the alternatives
before you will be stark – atomic extinction or the
unification of the world on the basis of some form
of dictatorship in which a rich and powerful minority
hold down a poor and powerless majority.

I do not believe this is what God intends the shape
of the future to be, nor is it the kind of world I want
you to inherit. So I must do what I can and put my
faith in you to do the rest.

Self-fulfilment

With some relief I turn from politics and philosophy
so that I can share with you more personal, intimate

107

thoughts before I end this letter which has mysteriously grown into a book.

I crave for each of you success, but I am fairly sure that my understanding of the term is different from the popular one. Has Kaunda been a success? The critics, commentators and historians will no doubt produce their measuring rods and size me up according to their definition of success. But I would claim that only Kaunda knows the real truth, not only because he is the only one who knows what goals he set himself and the extent to which he has achieved them, but even more important, only Kaunda knows *who* Kaunda is. Discard all the titles, medals and honours as fripperies and you are left with a human being who has finally only one ultimate power which depends on no one else and cannot be taken from him by anyone else – the power of self-fulfilment.

Self-fulfilment – that is what I understand by success. Every person has one aptitude within him. Nature has seen to that by evolving countless millions of human types none of whom is identical. Even in those totalitarian societies where the massed battalions of citizens wear identical uniforms, mouth the same slogans and march to the same beat, you can drill them until they turn and wheel and operate like one gigantic human organism, but the uniformity is an optical illusion. Each one has a secret, interior life. That is the gift of Nature which no political ideology can obliterate.

Learn this lesson well. Society will inevitably force certain conformities on you. It must: common systems of law, widely accepted customs and generally approved standards of behaviour are necessary to its operation.

Indeed, society must go further and by various
mechanisms encourage some degree of specialization.
It would be at best wasteful and at worst insane if
every man built his own house, wrote his own book,
cobbled his own shoes and dug his own copper. And
yet, however tightly organized the social unit, society
if it is to respond to the demands of Nature must
allow each of its citizens some degree of what I would
call psychic space – an area in which each one can
be his own man, think his own thoughts, speak his own
words and give expression to some inner drive which,
provided it is not evil, has the right to assert itself as
a bird has the right to fly.

In my view one of the curses of modern society
is that it tries to turn its members into either borrowers
or mimics. The young are conditioned to dress like
their favourite pop star, talk like some cinema hero
or heroine, read what every one else is reading and
think the mechanically or electronically propelled
thoughts of self-styled prophets of fashion, politics or
even religion. Yet the test of a free and mature society
is a simple one. Dare any member of it do what he
does best, with the necessary qualification that in doing
so he does not harm his neighbour?

Of course there are certain uniquely creative people.
There can only be one Homer, Shakespeare, Newton,
Gandhi. And it is one function of a mature society to
provide them with an environment which is hospitable
to the full blossoming of their gifts. Though I blush
to add myself to the roll of giants I have just named,
you will not, I'm sure, misunderstand me if I claim
that in Zambia there can only be one Kenneth Kaunda.
That is not a boast but a simple statement of fact. A

whole complex of factors thrust me to the forefront
of our national history at a crucial time. But I am
desperately anxious that you should not be either
influenced or intimidated by my reputation or position.
I don't want you all to live under my shadow or even
necessarily to walk in my direction. It may be that one
or more of you is unfortunate enough to have been
given an itch for politics. So be it; your poor mother
will have to make the best of a bad job in presiding
over a fireside or dinner table parliament. For the
rest, I want you to dare to be what you have it in you
to be. Believe me I shall glow with pride if you are able
to plough a straight furrow or bake a good loaf of
bread. Equally, I shall have failed if you feel you
must warp your personalities out of a false sense
of obligation to the Kaunda aura. When that great
Emperor and general, Alexander visited the philosopher, Diogenes, he asked if there was anything he
could do for him. 'Yes,' replied Diogenes, 'Stand
out of my light!' I have often thought of that reply.
It seems to me to express every person's obligation
to another – to avoid limiting his self-fulfilment. So I
want to stand out of your light so that you may achieve
self-fulfilment at your own pace and in your own way.

What I am really saying is that the ultimate difference
between success and failure has to do with one's
degree of self-trust, the confidence that God has given
you some gift which makes you who you are. It may
not be a gift of such a kind or magnitude that it
brings you into the public eye or inscribes your name
in the history books – that, after all, is small consolation
after you are dust. The most mediocre creature walking
our streets has one advantage denied to the greatest

personage of history. He is here! He can breathe and
laugh and love. And most important, he can do something well for its own sake. You know, I put great
store in the power of sheer enjoyment. It is one of the
most influential of all human drives. To do something
with zest for no other reason than that it pleases you
is a source of great power in the human personality.
I've read all about the moody genius, creating great
works of art in some attic and measuring his success
by the degree of misery he felt himself and imposed
on others. Well, if you turn out to be a moody genius,
I can only wish you well and take pride in you from
a safe distance. I must also, I suppose, take account
of those strange humans who confound my theory
by deriving huge enjoyment from inflicting pain on
others, putting one over their rivals in business, their
enjoyment expanding into bliss if they can manage
to bankrupt them in the process. But I am not prepared
to abandon my contention that sheer enjoyment is a
great source of fulfilment merely because there are
the odd exceptions whose idea of fun is tearing the
wings off butterflies.

I am equally convinced that, with the usual exceptions, the happy are also the good. The converse is
not, of course, true. Thank God for those sensitive
saints who enter into the sufferings and miseries of
their fellow human beings. They are certainly good
without being happy. Indeed, such spiritual giants
would pronounce it a great sin to be happy so long
as a single fellow human being is in pain, need or
adversity. That is what true religion is for, to raise us
above our natural state and inspire us to share what
God has given us with others. Yet there is such a

thing as a *natural* state, and this, I maintain, is the genuine goodness of the happy man or woman. Your grandmother, who died at the age of ninety, was a happy, good woman. Her needs were modest, and I'm afraid she found her politician son as much an embarrassment as a source of pride. She never really understood why protocol or security should require my visits to her little house to be so noisy and fussy. All those flashing blue lights on police cars, the long processions of Government land-rovers, the entourage of officials – they scared her chickens and I was always slightly afraid she would assault the Minister for the Nothern Province or shoo away the President of the Republic of Zambia for disturbing her peace! She taught me more than I can ever repay, and one thing in particular – that a life based upon *having* is less happy than one centred on *being* or *doing*. It is one of the less welcome legacies of Western influence in Africa that too many of our people have learned to elevate possessions above service and to regard position as more significant than usefulness.

There were times when I was most immersed in the intrigues and complexities of statecraft and surrounded by all the humming, pounding instruments of government, I would think of my old mother, sitting at the door of her little house, hens pecking away in the yard, the ageless cycle of growth, harvest and decay occurring all about her. She chatted to her friends and took life as it came, sunshine and storm, light and darkness. Nothing much happened to her, and yet in a real sense *everything* that matters happened to her. She knew what fulfilment was, and she was good because she was happy. Of course, it is hopeless

romanticism to imagine that we can ever put the clock
back and sweep away the complications and pressures
of modern life. There is no way back to the Garden
of Eden once we have eaten of the fruit of the tree of
knowledge. Yet I am convinced that my mother's
generation had much to teach us – that deep down life
is a matter of quality rather than quantity. Quantity
may be a factor beyond your control, for example, the
number of brain cells in your head or the amount of
money in the bank. But quality most certainly is not.
It can be a function of every single thing we do, no
matter how private or trivial. It is up to you whether
you do well or badly whatever duty or inclination
causes you to set your hand and brain to. Granted, the
pace of modern life often gives little scope for too
intense a concentration upon quality. There is so much
to do and so little time in which to do it. But one
thing, one thing we must do well – not because we
shall necessarily enrich the world but because our
self-respect and therefore our self-fulfilment depends
upon being able to acknowledge with quiet satisfaction
that whatever it is could not have been done better by
anybody else.

One of the glories of youth is health and vitality,
the gift of good eyesight, the ability to live long days,
to be almost impervious to physical discomfort. These
elemental human traits make possible a range and
scope of activities which inevitably narrow as our
physical faculties decline, our life-style becomes fixed,
our career imprisons us within a routine as rigid as an
iron cage. This is the inevitable price of maturity – loss
of variety, the dimming of wonder and narrowing of
perspective. Of all the interests we might have pursued,

we settle for a few: of all the people with whom we might associate, we select a small number. We become trapped in a web of fixed relationships. Hence youth is a vital time for experiment and exploration, for the exercise of that most important gift – the gift of curiosity. Why are things as they are? What is behind that closed door? What will happen if we do this rather than that? Most of the world's great discoveries and inventions have been almost byproducts of this faculty, the refusal to accept that things are immutably fixed and cannot be changed. I doubt that the great inventor necessarily sets out to produce that device with which his name is forever after associated. More often, he finds one thing when he is looking for another, or sometimes when he is looking for nothing in particular, merely asking himself what would happen if he refused to accept as axiomatic certain truths which had hitherto been beyond question.

I don't know whether the Kaunda family is likely to produce any great inventor or explorer, but I do hope that you will all develop open-mindedness to new possibilities; the ability to look at familiar things from an unusual angle. This is a quality which has as much relevance to the world of people as to the world of things. Your next-door neighbour, the student who sits next to you in the lecture room, the person who works at the next bench, the housewife you meet at the shop counter or market stall; all these and every other person who comes your way has an experience and a history worth exploring. They have known wonder and disappointment, pain and joy, success and failure. I want you to learn the wonder of the Other. For this is one of the great reasons for living – to discover the

114

truth and interest locked away in those with whom we are thrown into contact.

The people of the old Africa, of your grandmother's generation for example, had this faculty for showing a courteous curiosity about others. They would not pass a traveller on the road without greeting him, asking him his business and destination. Westerners tend to regard such curiosity as impertinence and invasion of privacy – but then they are capable of sitting in a train on their way to work every day for twenty years without doing more than wish their companions good morning. And what a lot they lose if they did but know it! This desire to share the wonder and excitement of another human being is one of the byproducts of Humanism. It is a practical demonstration of the truth of our essential unity. We belong to each other as people. There is no one so isolated that he cannot both give and receive comfort, inspiration or encouragement to at least a few others. I would go further and say that no one is granted by the Almighty a licence exempting him from his responsibilities as a member of the human race. And one such responsibility is to make himself available to others. This is the lesson of all great religions – the acceptance of claims against oneself which may involve time, money and energy but also offer in return enrichment of personality and Divine approval.

There is another lesson I wish to impress on you. At all costs have the courage to fail. That may seem a strange statement, but I am sure that one reason why mature people learn less than the young is that they are willing to risk less. Adult pride disposes us to avoid the humiliation of having to admit failure in any of our enterprises. Here, the child is wiser than the man. All children learn at a phenomenal rate because their pride is not at stake when they make mistakes. They attempt all kinds of things and are not particularly discouraged if they fail. But as we grow older, we all carry around with us in our heads a catalogue of things we have no intention of trying again because we attempted them once and failed.

We pay a heavy price for our fear of failure. It hinders our growth and narrows the range of our achievements. The great German poet, Goethe said men will go on making mistakes so long as they are striving after something. I could give you many examples from my own experience of this truth. In the history of Zambia's struggle for independence, the path was not straight and unimpeded by obstacles. Again and again I and my colleagues made attempts to win concessions from the Colonial Government. We tried this stategy and that, and some of our policies proved to be mistaken or inappropriate to that stage of our growth as a nationalist movement. But we had to go on trying, and failing, and trying again. There was no shortage of spectators who laughed cynically when we suffered setbacks. But eventually we were able to find a way round the formidable obstacles to our goal. I have no doubt that when the historians chronicle the story of Zambia's early years, they will be able to record instances of my own personal misjudgments of people and policy decisions of my Government which proved to have failed. But the point is that such successes as we have achieved are the necessary consequence of those failures. How can you know, for example, whether someone can be trusted with power unless you give him the chance to prove himself? It is one of the pecularities of politics as opposed to other fields of human endeavour that decisions are rarely self-evidently correct – they are only proved to be so when their consequences have been fully worked in the passage of time.

So, I beg of you, be prepared to have the courage to risk failure. Do not settle for safe courses of action which are almost certain to produce some modest degree of success if there is any possibility that a calculated risk may offer a greater prize. It takes more courage to risk failure than to achieve success. The acclaim of the crowd is always sweeter on the ears than its scorn. I have known both scorn and acclaim and though, like every human being, I prefer approval to unpopularity, I have learned the hard way that my greatest successes – in the sense of the things which have given me the most personal satisfaction – have been built on a foundation of failures which were necessary, though none the less unpalatable for that fact.

Once your formal schooling is over, the learning process will either stop or be restricted within narrow limits unless you are prepared to go on risking failure by trying new things, putting your trust in people who prove to be unknown quantities and exploring uncharted ways that may turn out to be dead ends or else open up new vistas of service and satisfaction. Always remember that parable of Jesus about the man who buried his master's money in the ground because he was afraid he might lose it if he took the chance of a risky investment. He was condemned precisely because he lacked the courage to risk failure. What applies to finance, has even greater relevance in

those momentous decisions which finally determine
the shape of our lives and the extent of our contribution
to human society.

Often as I travel round our country, I look from the
windows of my car or gaze at the assembled crowds
who come to greet me and hear me speak. I see a
citizen on a bicycle, a hoe over his shoulder, heading
for the fields, or a young woman, a baby on her back
chatting by the roadside, or a government official going
about his everyday business. I pass churches filled with
worshippers, shops packed with customers, processions
of men making their way to the factory gates or the
mine shaft, and I am filled with humility and respect.
For *they* are Zambia, and whether they know it or not,
the fate of this country is in their hands. I suppose men
of affairs such as myself are necessary to direct the
national effort, but it is the power and integrity of the
ordinary people who will finally decide our destiny.
Don't succumb to the heresy that it is only politicians,
industrialists and people of social importance who
determine either the tone or the quality of the nation.
Commitment is not the prerogative of the talented and
powerful. Every single person differs in the goals for
which he strives, and provided such goals fall within a
moral and political framework which is in line with
our national aspirations, then it is not for the Government or anyone else to discriminate between the
importance of the millionaire businessman and a peasant
farmer.

The West places great emphasis on individual
performance and loads honours on those who give
themselves to civic affairs, to great causes, to heroic
endeavours. Traditional societies such as ours put much

118

more stress on social cohesion. Many of the most valuable people in our societies do not burn with zeal for anything except the integrity, wellbeing and health of their own families. They don't seek to revolutionize the character of their own village, let alone the world, and we value them for the contribution they make to our national wellbeing just by strengthening family life. In the end, the nation is only as healthy, strong and vital as its basic unit – the family.

So I shall weep no tears if the extent of your contribution to Zambia does not shake the nation by its power. A wise man once said that every calling is great when greatly pursued. And the noblest calling of all is to be true to oneself, to find fulfilment in something which one does well, and to help nourish the sinews of a healthy family. You are not condemned to be a small-scale individual simply because you live in a small-scale community and share the daily toil of your fellow-citizens. Just see to it that you stretch yourself at some point so that your reach always exceeds your grasp. Dream a little, live in hope of better things for your children than you yourselves enjoyed. And above all else, don't become one of those moaners who would find something about which to complain in the Garden of Eden. Think affirmatively, and remember that it is always easier to destroy than to build up. It takes no great ingenuity to find fault with others, to dishearten them and lay bare their blemishes. But to think well of others, to encourage them in well-doing, to help them to conquer their weaknesses and develop their hidden potentialities – that is the attitude and vocation of a true Humanist.

Courage in face of fear

What else has my life taught me that I am anxious to
pass on to you? Possibly something about courage.
Every sensible person knows fear. Indeed, I have
learned that fear has a creative role in the development
of the human personality. Granted, fear can be a
shattering emotion, confusing judgment, paralysing
effort, displacing faith by cynicism and hope by dismay.
Yet, if you think about it, behind every great human
achievement there stands a real fear. The glories of
medical science may derive in part from the compassion
and brilliance of scientific minds, but there is, behind
every conquest of disease, a primitive fear of what a
disease can do to the human organism. We rightly extol
the great pioneers of education whose positive motivation was to help every child achieve the potential
within him. Such aspirations were the 'pull' of educational advance, but the 'push' of it was fear of illiteracy
and ignorance – the demon possession of minds by
superstition and dark forces which only the light of
knowledge could banish.

Fear is, in fact, an instructor, a warning and a driving
force which can be used to advantage. It is a lesson
both of history and of personal experience that we often
only value things when we are threatened by their loss.
We take the support and love of others for granted
until that dark moment arrives when we may lose
them. A nation enjoys freedom and gives little thought
to the wonder of it until the people are crushed under
the heel of a conqueror. A man assumes justice to be

his right until the cell door unjustly clangs shut on
him. So I would claim that he who knows no fear is
more likely to be stupid than brave. This world is not
all sweetness and light; it has its harsh, dangerous
aspects also, and if a man is wise, there are things that
he will fear in the very depths of his being – atomic
extinction, political oppression, economic injustice – to
mention only three scourges of the modern world.

So I would not wish any of you to become idiot-
heroes, capable of daring deeds because you lack the
sensitivity to know what is at stake in the challenges
you face. And yet such fears must be conquered if we
are not to live, quivering and afraid, in some dark
corner, hoping that we may pass unnoticed when heroic
action is demanded of us.

For what it is worth, my own experience has been
this. The most potent constituent of fear is ignorance
and the greatest antidote against it is knowledge. I
vividly recall the first occasion I found myself in conflict
with the law. My legs trembled the first time a police-
man put his hand on my shoulder, the first time I stood
in the dock facing a magistrate who took away my
freedom, the first time I heard the door of a prison cell
lock behind me. Before the freedom struggle was over,
I was an old lag of such experience and I could have
taught the police a thing or two about the law. Each
time I had to face a fearful situation, the knowledge
that I had been there before lessened my terror and
enabled me to control my panic and get things
into perspective. I hasten to add that I am not now
advocating that you ought to precipitate a brush
with the law in order to overcome your fear of the
unknown! I really hope that you will never need to

fear the law because your conduct doesn't bring you
into collision with it. But I hope you get my basic
point. We all, rightly, fear the unknown, and the
most potent element in the unknown is imaginative
anticipation. You probably discovered this the first time
you had to visit a dentist. You felt the pain long
before you entered his surgery. I still shudder a little
when I see that formidable array of surgical instruments
in the dentist's consulting room! But experience, and
therefore knowledge, has taught me that there are few
fears in this life which are as terrifying in reality as we
imagine them to be in anticipation.

Fear is relative. The child in a darkened bedroom is
as terrified of a fluttering moth as a soldier is of the
barrel of his enemy's machine gun. So courage has
much to do with directness. If something is both
inevitable and terrifying it is better, if possible, to face
it now, rather than live through the fear a dozen
times in the imagination. The real sting of fear is
illusion. Some men of arms have been defeated long
before they stand face to face with their enemy. The
first time I found myself at a political meeting facing
the Mobile Unit of the old Northern Rhodesia Police
which had been detailed to round us up, each of those
steel-helmeted, heavily armed policemen seemed at least
eight feet tall. In time I came to learn that not only
were they human beings like myself but also that they
were at least as scared of me as I was of them.

I also learned something else of great importance –
courage is contagious. Just as panic rapidly spreads
through a crowd when one or two members lose
their self-control and begin to dash for safety, so
one courageous individual can instil the virtue in

his jittery companions. I love that story of George
Washington, who in the desperate days of the Revolu-
tionary War in America, reviewed a fresh contingent
of raw recruits from Connecticut, badly equipped
and terrified of the disciplined British Army they were
shortly to face. Washington scanned their tattered
ranks and said, 'I have great confidence in you men of
Connecticut'. And according to the historian who
recorded this incident, more than one of those recruits
wept and clasping his musket in his arms swore he
would do his best to justify Washington's confidence in
him.

Well, I'm not George Washington, but I also have
great confidence in you and I pray that each of you
will become a rallying point of courage in a nation
which is beset with so many perils that from time to
time the nerve of many of our citizens is bound to
fail. It was a great American President, Franklin D.
Roosevelt who once said, 'The only thing we have
to fear is fear itself!' I believe that fervently. Our
technical problems are soluble, our relations with
neighbouring countries whose philosophies are
antagonistic to ours will stabilize, given patience and
steadfastness. What we need for our survival and
victory is a commodity in short supply – the courageous
individual citizen who has cool nerves and a combination
of national pride and self-respect. The biggest handicap
we face in overcoming the birth-pangs of nationhood, I
would locate in neither the area of politics, economics
or social development. It is the *small-scale individual* who
in a time of immense peril and opportunity fails to
recognize that his greatest contribution to our nationhood is to stand by the best he knows, to match fear

with knowledge, and catch a glimpse of a vision of
what the nation of Zambia could become, given the
simplest of human virtues courageously upheld in
whatever situation, great or humble, a man finds himself.

Man and Nature

Having spent a rare weekend in the country, getting
rid of some of my surplus weight and toning up my
muscles by digging in my garden, I'm inspired to reflect
on the joys of the open air and the delights and
satisfactions of tilling the land. It may seem odd to you
that I think such a traditional part of African life
worth making the subject of comment and advice. But
I foresee a time when the growth of our cities and the
constant movement of people from the land to the
towns may cause yours and succeeding generations to
look upon the peasantry as an inferior species of
citizen. Paradoxically, in the industrialized West, land
is at such a premium that the landowner is often a
person of wealth and consequence. But Zambia has
over a quarter of a million square miles of largely
uncultivated bush. And if you turn your backs upon
the pastoral heritage of your ancestors and become
underexercised town-dwellers whose children believe
that milk comes from a dairy and vegetables from the
market, you will lose something precious, something
that links you with mankind from the dawn of time.

The first man was the first farmer. Of all professions
this is the one which stands nearest to God, for this
was the original calling of the human race. I confess
when I was a boy and had to spend my school holidays

in the fields or tending the cattle and poultry, I thought it a burdensome chore to be put behind me as soon as I could qualify to be a teacher, a clerk; someone whose place was at a desk, harvesting paper and garnering into filing cabinets. It is only since I have found myself imprisoned within four walls, surrounded as far as the eye can see with great buildings, busy roads and the clatter of the city that I have come to realize what a profound philosophy of life and what great satisfaction and wisdom are derived from the relationship between man and the land.

The man on the land may have to bend to the law of the country and the edicts of Government, but he has also to accommodate himself to the more elemental laws represented by the order of the seasons, the vagaries of the weather and those forces of Nature which he cannot control but may be able to use. In the city it is the clock that calls the tune to which a man must dance, and a frenzied and often joyless pace it is. But the man on the land must accept the imposition upon him of the rhythm of nature, adjusting himself to a cycle of sowing, growing and harvesting that he can neither hurry nor delay. Nature determines her own working day, and she never hurries – atom by atom, little by little her task is achieved. She is a mistress who demands patience and teaches it by manipulating sun and wind, flood and drought. And she builds men to her own pattern and for her own uses. They may know nothing of the workings of the internal combustion engine, the miracles of television and the telephone, never travel through the air at the speed of sound, but at least they eat plain, fresh food, sleep well, breathe pure air and grow strong muscles.

125

I see a great parable in Nature that we acquisitive men of the town would do well to study. We can create our great industrial and commercial enterprises and within a generation by our folly or evil intent liquidate them so that there is only a ruin or even a mountain of debt to pass on to those who come after us. But Nature doesn't allow such piracy. Like a cautious man of wealth she ties up her estate in such a way that no one generation can squander it. So long as a man has a handful of seed, a bucket of water and the capacity for work he will always find wealth in the land one year or one generation later. But he must learn dependence, and adjust his life to accept with equanimity both the blessings and curses of Nature. The sun which exhausts him also brings up the corn. The rivers which wash away his soil compensate him by giving him fish. The trees which keep the lifegiving sun and rain from his growing crops, can still be chopped down to keep him warm on cold nights.

I have no ambition or talent to become a homespun country philosopher; I merely wish to draw your attention to the obvious. Whatever Zambia lacks, she does not lack land. Whatever trade, profession or vocation you decide to follow, I hope you will keep an intense interest in land to which you can retire when the pace of life in the modern city becomes intolerable. It will slow the beat of your heart, increase the capacity of your lungs, force patience on the most restless of you and dependence on the proudest. It is no false romanticism I'm foisting on to you. I'm well aware of the cruelties and treacheries of Nature. But there is also a wisdom to be acquired away from the artificialities of city life which I venture to think you may profit by.

Thoughts on immortality

I must now take a firm grip on myself and bring these
random thoughts to a close; but not without some
statement of my deepest convictions about the single
most important fact about you and every other human
being – the certainty of immortality.

I write these words in a time of personal bereavement.
Your grandmother was, it is true, ninety years of
age and so it is foolish to grieve too much over a
quiet end to a full and happy life. But the death of
someone precious to us, whatever their age or manner
of dying, must lead to some questioning about immortality. Surely, this is the question which has been most
commonly asked in the entire history of the world:
does anything come after this life? Is that tiny span of
existence between conception and death all there is;
after which, darkness and utter obliteration?

As a Humanist, I am convinced that the destiny of
Man is not limited to his existence on earth and he
must never lose sight of this fact or else he devalues
his essential nature. Leaving aside for a moment the
dogmatic statements of the great religions, especially
Christianity, about the reality of eternal life, there seem
to be certain commonsense pointers to our abiding
existence which can be detected within our own
experience and by elementary observation. Man, I
think, continues to exist less by the actions he performs
during his life than by the trail or wake he leaves
behind him like the track of a shooting star. He may
be unaware of it himself and be convinced that death

I

closes the book for ever. But I am convinced that death is the beginning of a greater and more significant reality.

Consider the disproportion between the biological duration of a person's life and the extent of his influence on future generations. I am not now thinking of the vast tide of influence left behind them by a Moses, a Buddha, a Confucius or a Christ. The power of their continuous example has helped to construct the unalterable framework of our moral life. It is no daring assertion to claim that they never die. But what of the unknown masses, the uncounted millions who die unmourned except for a tiny group of kinsfolk and friends? The world seems to grind on as though they had never been. What of them?

I would make the same assertion that their influence is an abiding one. Consider the case of my old mother. By her character, example and opinions, she left an indelible mark on her family and friends. Her memory will persist long after she has gone; her words and behaviour will inspire people whom she never knew. That which was best in her, which she gave sometimes unconsciously to those around her, will never die completely. For all I know, there are people who have had the patience to spend the odd hour considering these thoughts of mine, who, if anything I have written has been of modest value, have through me had their lives touched by the influence of my parents.

For the Humanist, the evolution of the spirit blazes on in the trail which a man leaves behind him and which widens or prolongs the trace others have left and so contributes to its fanlike expansion. This is a kind of personal immortality of which we can be sure even if we are agnostic (which I am not) about the more dogmatic pronouncements of Christianity. It is the excitement and satisfaction of being part of the great procession of mankind. The very first man who buried his child in grief and did not leave his body to the mercy of some scavenging animal but built a pile of stones over the place; the first man who decreed that the wounded, the old and incapacitated should not be left to die but should be fed; the first man who forbade his children to kill their fellow men; the first man to scrawl on the walls of a cave or make weird musical sounds – the influence of all such human pioneers is still with us and we have entered into their inheritance. We are linked to our remotest ancestors by an immaterial but unbroken thread. And if we are wise, gratitude will be one element of that thread. We are who we are, and not worse than we are, because of alien and foreign beings, long gone in the mists of time, who in their wildest imaginings could never have dreamt of a world such as ours.

From all of this you will gather that your father is an incurable and unrepentant romantic. But better to have such a colourful view of our origins and past than that of those gloomy and ultimately despairing philosophers who see the lives of even their nearest and dearest as a mere shadow, a flicker on a vast, dark backdrop; one moment here, the next gone. Not only do such pessimists deprive themselves of comfort in the interests of what they call realism but they end up by devaluing Man, and so provide the raw material of Fascist ideologies.

No, I cling firmly to the conviction that no man ever disappears completely if he strives to do good and expects no reward outside the joy of having contributed to the progress of mankind. What is the point of our scientific genius, our technological brilliance, if they do not lead Man to a better comprehension of himself, of the meaning of his life, and of the resources buried in his inner self?

The conquest of Nature alone cannot bring Man the happiness he has the right to expect, unless there is some corresponding moral development which must come, in the last resort, from a true valuation of himself, and also from a reconciliation of the rational – science – with the irrational – faith. It is from a harmonizing of the roles of Man as animal, the prisoner of his instincts, with Man as Spirit, free-roaming and capable of non-natural acts of sacrifice and love, that a philosophy must eventually evolve which may make the world a safer, more beautiful and happier place for your children's children to inherit.

In those inevitable moods of despondency and impotence, you must never forget that you are heirs to all the spiritual treasures of mankind and keepers of an eternal flame which the greatest and purest of men from time immemorial have passed on to you. That flame has burned on over the decay of civilizations, the devastations of war and the chaos of natural disasters.

The Humanist's view of the future

The Humanist has great hope for the future of mankind, but he is not an optimist in the sense that he imagines things automatically getting better by some evolutionary process or historical drive that is carrying

us onwards and upwards. I detect no signs that the
world will, in the most fundamental sense, be a better
place in your time than it was in mine. Scientifically,
certainly, one would expect many natural hazards,
ranging from incurable diseases to the destructive
forces of Nature, to be eliminated. But Man's fundamental problem is an *internal* one, and until he develops
the wisdom to recognize this fact he will cast about
him in ever increasing desperation for the key which
unlocks the outer gates of Utopia.

In all his relations with his fellows, Man must use
his reason, that is why God endowed him with it, but
he will perpetrate fewer errors if he listens to his heart.
In the everyday commerce of human life it is better to
be generous than just, to sympathize rather than try to
understand what is irrational in human behaviour.
Whether or not you have been convinced by your
upbringing and the teachings of the Church that there
is a God above who created and sustains us, it is always
better to stand for truth against error, love rather than
hate, service in preference to selfishness, sacrifice in
place of self-preservation. For these are the qualities
which finally change the world for the better, and it is
a deeply satisfying thing to know that you have left the
world, your society and generation a little better than
you found them.

Nations, as well as individuals, ought to know what
they want. If countries want peace they must understand that the problem in essence is not one of treaties,
world organizations or codes of international law.
Peace must first of all be established by transforming
Man from within. The source of all evil, all wars, all
injustice, lies within us. It is not 'out there' in the

egotism of the super-powers or even in the arrogance
of small nations who compensate for their military and
economic weaknesses by a foolhardy determination to
assert themselves at whatever cost to their people. The
real enemy has occupied not the top of our minds in
vain imaginings but the bottom of hearts in devilish
pride.

Yes, the old man is preaching at you again. But take
it as a compliment that I believe in you and your
generation sufficiently to hope that you may be preserved
from repeating endlessly the same old errors and evils
which have torn the world apart, not once but twice in
living memory. I am greatly encouraged by the
sharpened conscience of the young. When one has given
full weight to the gloomy head-shakings and expressions
of disapproval of senior generations, I still believe that
the young people of our world are not necessarily
doomed to become the cynical and time-serving old.
They *care* about poverty and discrimination and
injustice, and though their protests may occasionally
take somewhat bizarre forms, they see further and feel
more deeply than many of my own generation. It is
not quite so easy to get them to bow down before
the gods of materialism and security. They have
a sense of the reality of the spirit world even though
they demonstrate it in dangerous ways such as the
attempt to deepen their consciousness by the use
of the drugs, the pursuit of various forms of world-
denying mysticism, and a choice of heroes who may
prove to have not only feet of clay but heads filled with
cotton wool.

We start the process of recreating the world right
where we are, not thousands of miles distant in the

UN Headquarters or even further away at the frontiers of outer space. My own conversion to Humanism dates from the time when I realized that the things which unite men are more important and enduring than the things which divide them. And I began my crusade within the narrow confines of our own nation by trying to get sufficient of our people to recognize that tribal and racial divisions are a basic denial of that essential humanity which we share with all who live and breathe, know truth, feel the pangs of conscience and share a common goal. After all, what does it matter whether you shoot a zebra through one of his black stripes rather than the white? He bleeds to death just the same.

So I have become, as my father was, an evangelist, proclaiming the dignity of Man, whether he occupies a grass hut in the wilds of Africa or a penthouse flat in New York or Moscow. I am impervious to the sneers of my detractors or the attacks of my intellectual superiors. I know *what* I know, not from the top of my head but from the bottom of my heart. Cleverness, ingenuity and worldly wisdom have not taken us one step nearer the goal of world peace and human brotherhood. It is time we tried goodness. Jesus said it two thousand years ago, and he has yet to be proved wrong.

My more candid friends tell me that I am living a dream and chasing a ghost along a rainbow. They may be right. But I shall struggle on, preaching the simplest and most fundamental of all truths: that in the end, beneath all the technicalities of world or national problems, it is the quality of the individual who finally decides the destiny of the State and beyond, the fate of the world. There is nothing which can

claim permanence in this life except that which takes
up its home in the consciousness of the individual.
Governments rise and fall, cities sprout and decay, the
scientific truths of one generation are proved to be
errors by the next. Only Man is capable of constant
spiritual evolution. And even he may well come to a
sudden catastrophic end unless he learns the elementary
lesson that in a nuclear age the whole world is the
smallest unit of survival. 'Mankind' is now a reality
because the alternative is unthinkable. But this is not
good enough. Though deterrents have a place in
human affairs by forcing men to do unwillingly what
they will not do for choice, I cannot believe that Man
was intended to survive against the threat of dark,
sinister realities. For this is to make fear his dominant
emotion and most powerful motivating force. What
place, then, in such a world have joy, beauty and truth?
Are they just diversions, the ornamental decorations on
the coffin of humanity?

At the present time, everybody is quite rightly
preoccupied with the organization of the world peace.
All are agreed that this is the problem which over-
shadows all others. But we argue endlessly about
'external' solutions. We talk of treaties, conventions,
courts of arbitration, *detentes*, international agreements.
All very necessary I am sure, but in the absence of
respect, integrity and good faith, such instruments are
merely pieces of paper, and whoever heard of a piece of
paper that could stop a bullet? The effectiveness of all
such artifacts depends on the moral character of the
men who have drafted them and solemnly agreed to
uphold them.

The problem of peace is far too grave and complex

to be solved by diplomatic machinery, however
elaborate. It will only be solved when children such
as yourselves are taught from an early age that the
English, Chinese, South Africans, Russians, Americans
or whatever, are not impersonal enemies or evil ogres—
they are people entitled to dignity and respect, who
love their children, their families and their countries,
who feel as we feel, fear what we fear and hope as we
hope, for a world in which no needless blood is spilt
and where the resources that God has given to all men
will be shared by all.

If such sentiments are dismissed as hopeless idealism,
then so be it. But I am not prepared to base either my
own philosophy of life or that which I pass on to my
children on the premise that Man is a bloodthirsty
brute, motivated only by greed and arrogance. I want
you all to think well of your fellow men. Of course
you will, from time to time, be disillusioned and even
hurt when you are let down; when your trust in another
human being is repaid by treachery. But it is still
better to give another human being the opportunity to
rise to your highest expectations of him than to make
it a policy to assume the worst in order that you may
never be disappointed. That may be the path of
prudence but it is a violation of the truth that there is a
divine spark in every man to which it is always worth
appealing before one must protect oneself from his
vicious instincts. Better by far to know both the joy
and pain of honest human encounter than to construct
a shell which may make you impervious to hurt but
also keeps out that searching love which I choose to
believe even the most miserable men may be seeking to
express, however tentatively.

The spirit of youth

I remind myself of one of my father's sermons. He was
a great preacher, though sometimes he went on a little
too long for us children who did not really understand
the importance of what he was saying. Whenever he
came to the point where he paused and said, 'and now,
lastly . . .', we knew that meant there was at least
another twenty minutes to go, for he found the truth of
the Gospel inexhaustible and couldn't resist adding a
little more to the sermon, and more, and more . . .

Well, I have finished now. I and my generation aged
before our time. We were agitators in our early teens,
arguing constitutional matters with Colonial Secretaries
and Governors in our early twenties and a few years
later we had laid on us the responsibility for governing
a new nation. So we didn't get much time in which to
be young. So I would urge you all not to be too
anxious to put youth behind you. You will, after all, be
old for a long time, and dead even longer. So keep alive
the spirit of youth for as long as you are able. Of
course, the pressures of time cannot be denied. We like
to think they can, and whilst we still burst with youthful
enthusiasm and idealism look upon our elders with
some degree of pity, swearing we will make a better job
of things than they did. But almost before we know it,
our arteries have begun to harden, our judgment
becomes more cautious and our behaviour more
measured, and behold! we find bounding up behind us
another generation as impatient of our attitudes as we
were of those of our elders.

It is a commonplace sneer of the older generation
that the young will soon learn to moderate their wild
emotions and passionate devotion to heroic causes once
they have married, settled down and have families to
support and some degree of security to achieve. But I
do not see that this is inevitable. The essential qualities
of youth – readiness for change, generosity of spirit,
impatience of hyprocrisy and cant, willingness to take
risks – have never been more needed than at this
juncture in history when the human race finds itself at a
crossroads. In one direction there lurks across our path
a new barbarism, none the less deadly because it has
the power of science and technology to fuel the engines
of its destructiveness. In another direction, there
beckons the shadowy outline of world community – a
goal far beyond us at present and cut off from us by
barriers which the generations senior to yours have
pronounced insurmountable. This I cannot and will not
believe. Certainly, in a single generation, you will not
be able to unite the shattered fragments of a bitterly
divided world and from them create an earthly paradise.
But provided you do not allow yourselves to become
discouraged by the smallness of the success you are able
to achieve before the world-weariness of middle and
old age settles upon you like a black cloud you will
have made life a little better for all who come after
you. Possibly the most serious enemy you will have to
overcome, fearsome because it is insidious and creeps
up imperceptibly, is nostalgia – the feeling that old
virtues are disappearing, old values disintegrating, and
the good old stern morality no longer honoured. Always
view with some suspicion those who contrast the good
old days with the evil and dissolute present. Take my

word for it, the people who prate on and on about the
good old days are likely to be suffering from defective
memories and would almost certainly refuse any
invitation to return to the past if science were to evolve
a Time Machine that made such journeys possible. The
good old days were not without their graciousness and
quiet joy but for the mass of mankind they were grim
and brutal. So be kind and generous in your judgment
of people who locate the Golden Age in the past, but
don't be taken in by them. Even when the ghastly toll
of this century's wars, disasters, civil disorders and
the human miseries which are a consequence of them,
has been added up and faced with a shudder, it is still
true that you have been born in an age which offers
greater opportunities for personal fulfilment and
human service than any which has preceded it.

It is one of those obvious and easily ignored lessons
of Nature which applies equally to human society – that
birth is always conquering death; that out of decay
there springs renewal. Of course none of those shining
values by which we set such store when young survives
for long without becoming encrusted with layers of
cynicism. It is of the nature of Man to desert the truth
and dash off in pursuit of some novel error. Yet there
is constancy as well as renewal in God's world. There
are those who hold fast to what is good whilst others
achieve new spiritual insights by their courage in
exploring unfamiliar paths. So the world is a great
seething, bubbling cauldron of essences both poisonous
and health-giving. Life is never as bad as the old fear
or the young believe. So avoid both cynical pessimism
and facile optimism and discover some hard realism for
yourselves. Don't worry too much about setting the

whole universe to rights, just try to make sense of that little patch in which God has placed you and do *something* with it. I've lived long enough to realize that the Golden Age about which we all dream and for which some of us strive is not a static state of bliss where all human problems will be resolved and mankind will live, like the virtuous ones in the fairy story – happily ever after. The Golden Age never dawns and yet paradoxically is always dawning when individuals are prepared to become agents of renewal and bearers of it. Remember Jesus's parable of the yeast in the dough. It works secretly and at a thousand separate points, transforming the lump, atom by atom. To the casual observer nothing much seems to be happening. Then, suddenly, through the sum total of countless isolated efforts everything is changed.

So I wish you cool nerves, sound judgment and strong constitutions. I envy you the age into which you will come to maturity and pray you may match its opportunities with your moral stature. I hope you will know happiness but not so much of it that you become complacent. And above all, I desire that you should be inheritors of a land and a world in whose challenges you will recognize not merely a burdensome responsibility but also a summons to greatness.

And one other thing . . . I hope you will have the good sense not to take too much notice of the gratuitous advice heaped upon you by old fogeys like me!